# Growing Together in Faith

**Emma**
This book is dedicated to all those who nurtured my faith as a child, especially my parents, David and Sheila, my sister Helen, and those who first welcomed me as a teenager at St Gabriel's Church. It is also dedicated to my husband James and daughter Sophie. Their endless supply of love and care (and not forgetting James's provision of fresh coffee) has encouraged me on this journey of writing. Thank you.

**Sarah**
This book is dedicated to my beautiful boys, Zach and Toby, who are my joy and inspiration. To my husband, Matt, who gifts me with love, patience and laughter every day. And finally, to my parents, Jane and Keith, who have supported me in every way possible.

# Growing Together in Faith

*Thinking Theologically about Ministry with Children and Teenagers*

Emma L. Parker and Sarah Strand

scm press

© Emma L. Parker and Sarah Strand 2025

Published in 2025 by SCM Press

Editorial office
3rd Floor, Invicta House,
110 Golden Lane,
London EC1Y 0TG, UK
www.scmpress.co.uk

SCM Press is an imprint of Hymns Ancient & Modern Ltd
(a registered charity)

Hymns Ancient & Modern® is a registered trademark of
Hymns Ancient & Modern Ltd
13A Hellesdon Park Road, Norwich,
Norfolk NR6 5DR, UK

All rights reserved. No part of this publication may be reproduced,
stored in a retrieval system, or transmitted,
in any form or by any means, electronic, mechanical,
photocopying or otherwise, without the prior permission of
the publisher, SCM Press.

The Author has asserted their right under the Copyright, Designs and
Patents Act 1988 to be identified as the Author of this Work

British Library Cataloguing in Publication data

A catalogue record for this book is available
from the British Library

ISBN: 978-0-334-06652-1

Except where indicated, Scripture quotations are from the New Revised Standard Version of the Bible, copyright 1989 by the Division of Christian Education of the National Council of the Churches of Christ in the USA. Used by permission. All rights reserved.

Where indicated, Scripture quotations marked (NIV) are taken from the Holy Bible, New International Version®, NIV®. Copyright © 1973, 1978, 1984, 2011 by Biblica, Inc.™ Used by permission of Zondervan. All rights reserved worldwide. www.zondervan.com. The "NIV" and "New International Version" are trademarks registered in the United States Patent and Trademark Office by Biblica, Inc.™

No part of this book may be used or reproduced in any manner for the purpose
of training artificial intelligence technologies or systems.

EU GPSR Authorised Representative
LOGOS EUROPE, 9 rue Nicolas Poussin, 17000, LA ROCHELLE, France
E-mail: contact@logoseurope.eu

Typeset by Regent Typesetting

# Contents

| | |
|---|---|
| *List of Abbreviations* | vii |
| *Acknowledgements* | ix |
| *Foreword* | xi |
| Introduction | 1 |
| 1 The Importance of Children and Teenagers: Digging Deeper into Theology<br>*Emma L. Parker* | 5 |
| 2 Exploring How Faith Grows: The Significance of Community<br>*Sarah Strand* | 18 |
| 3 The Whole People of God: Old and New Testament Insights<br>*Emma L. Parker* | 38 |
| 4 Intergenerational Church: Learning and Growing Together<br>*Emma L. Parker* | 54 |
| 5 Intergenerational Worship, Ministry and Vocation: Being Transformed Together<br>*Emma L. Parker* | 71 |
| 6 Households: Encountering Faith Together<br>*Sarah Strand* | 87 |

7  School Communities: Listening to the Voices of
   Children and Teenagers                                102
   *Sarah Strand*

8  Navigating Change: A Theological and Practical
   Model of Change for Growth                            117
   *Emma L. Parker*

Concluding Thoughts                                      134

*Index of Biblical References*                           139

# List of Abbreviations

*All Bible references are taken from the New Revised Standard Version (NRSV), unless otherwise indicated.*

| | |
|---|---|
| Genesis | Gen. |
| Exodus | Ex. |
| Deuteronomy | Deut. |
| Joshua | Josh. |
| 1 Samuel | 1 Sam. |
| 2 Samuel | 2 Sam. |
| 2 Chronicles | 2 Chron. |
| Psalm | Ps. |
| Isaiah | Isa. |
| Nehemiah | Neh. |
| Matthew | Matt. |
| Romans | Rom. |
| 1 Corinthians | 1 Cor. |
| 2 Corinthians | 2 Cor. |
| Galatians | Gal. |
| Ephesians | Eph. |
| Philippians | Phil. |
| Colossians | Col. |
| 1 Thessalonians | 1 Thess. |
| 1 Timothy | 1 Tim. |

# Acknowledgements

## Emma

I'm very grateful to those who have taught me so much about growing in faith with children and teenagers, especially Dave Ross, Jane Grieve and Andrea Swift. I am particularly thankful for Andrea, whose teaching, leadership, and passion for children, faith, school and church is utterly inspiring. Thanks also goes to Ethna Parker for her time and skill in reading my draft chapters, and to Emily and her daughter Lydia, for their joy, wisdom and encouragement. And finally, to all the children and teenagers who have taught me about the kingdom and enabled my faith to grow: thank you.

## Sarah

I'm so grateful for the support of the staff and students of Cranmer Hall, St John's College, Durham, and especially that of Lizzie Hare, Josh Cockayne, Nick Moore, Sam Tranter and Ian Galloway. Thank you to the Church of England's *Growing Faith Foundation* that generously funded the Growing Faith Learning Hub based at Cranmer Hall, which enabled the research in Chapter 7. I'm also grateful for the energy, passion and enthusiasm of Ana Moskvina, Claire Lewis and Grace Volans who assisted with the research. We have been privileged to meet with, and listen to, countless children and teenagers as we have prepared for this book. Thank you to each of you for sharing with us with such honesty, for asking such amazing questions and for causing us to reflect, wonder and change. We're so excited for the futures each of you will have and the way you will continue to shape and lead your churches and communities into the future.

# Foreword

When you ask us questions, sometimes we might not know the answer, but we know that we want something different than what's happening. So we do need a lot of your help rather than just us kind of making a lot of the decisions. We do need help and guidance on that journey.

So said a 13-year-old student in a conversation about the need for adults to listen to young people. The statement is both inarticulate and profoundly clear. Her words express the frustration of a young person of faith and the longing for something better. She asks for companionship and patience, for space to risk and fail and try again together. Her words demonstrate the tension of knowing something is wrong but not yet knowing what that is. There is a humility in acknowledging the need for help from adults as well as the passionate desire for change from what adults have created. It is the space between what is and what could be that is explored in this book, *Growing Together in Faith*.

I lead the Growing Faith Foundation, which started as a vision in 2019 and has grown to be a movement inspiring and enabling churches, schools and households to connect and grow faith across all ages, especially our children and young people. Growing Faith has been described as more of a 'lens' or a 'posture' than a bandwagon to jump on or a 'shiny new thing' to despise or delight in. In the forest imagery so engagingly explored in this book, Growing Faith is more of a mycorrhizal fungus than a majestic oak. It works quietly and unspectacularly underground, connecting and serving the beauty and fruitfulness of the biodiversity above the surface. Through the Growing Faith movement, the church is trying to inspire local spaces where young people like this teenager can experience the joy of belonging to a faith community that encourages them, supports them and resources them in their relationship with God, in their searching and questioning. A community that loves them unconditionally, mirroring the unconditional love of God for each of God's children. A community that celebrates their purpose and status as fellow disciples and prioritizes their needs just as much as the needs of all the other groups who are part of that local community of faith. Growing Faith is about noticing the importance, not only of churches in the faith formation of under-16-year-olds, but of the schools where our young people spend so much of their time and where their characters and attitudes are formed. Growing Faith also explores the importance of households and the vital roles that carers and parents play in the faith development of their children. It is rooted in listening to the dioceses and in the prayer of a cohort of supporters who faithfully pray for the work every week. It's increasingly about finding ways to help young people make their voice heard. The interviews carried out among under-16-year-olds as part of the Growing Faith Hub described in this book acknowledge that we need to listen attentively, rather than decide unilaterally what is good for people very different from us. Throughout the book, I was delighted (and unsurprised) to have the sense of writers who really listen to children: to what Scriptures are trying to say about children, to their own children, to those of the intergenerational community of the theological college, as well as to the children approached more formally during the research interviews. Not forgetting the reflective listening of the authors themselves on their own experience of childhood, parenthood and what it means to both belong to and lead a church that values children.

   I had the privilege of meeting Emma and Sarah early on in my work with the Growing Faith Foundation when they were both based at Cranmer Hall, a theological college in the north-east of England. Cranmer Hall has played an important part in shaping Growing Faith from the very beginning: Emma championed the Growing Faith vision here as soon as it was launched, wrote the first Growing Faith module and was on the interview panel for

## FOREWORD

the role I subsequently took up, while both Emma and Sarah later arranged for Cranmer ordinands to be part of the interview process for other roles on our team. It was Emma's passionate and spontaneous outburst on a videoconference about the importance of academic theological insights in the field of children's and youth ministry that led us to host the first Growing Faith research conference at Cranmer in 2023, at which both Sarah and Emma spoke with the rigour and wisdom that shine out throughout this book. Sarah headed up the Growing Faith Hub that drew together the rich vein of data for Chapter 7 and, at the time of writing, Cranmer is still the only theological training college that has a baked-in Growing Faith module for all its ministry students. This demonstrates the college's huge commitment to the principle of placing the child at the centre so that the culture of the church changes to become a more flourishing, intergenerational faith community; in Sarah's dynamic image, a forest where all species are interconnected and the organism as a whole is supportive of both older and newer forms of life.

Reading this book is rather like having extra members of the team throwing their sympathetic but rigorous expertise into the field, determined that together we can make even more of a cultural change within the church in the service of the kingdom. From the opening words of a child's questioning, 'Why?' to the final exploration of navigating change for and with not just children but the whole faith community in prayer together, we are taken step by step into a better understanding of what it means to place the child in the midst of all our faith communities. My hope and expectation is that this book will help students, church leaders, congregation members and other lifelong learners be even more convinced theologically, intellectually and emotionally to place children and young people at the heart of all we do as a church and to keep on making the necessary changes together with them and for everyone's sake: *we know that we want something different from what's happening.*

Lucy Moore
Head of the Growing Faith Foundation

# Introduction

This is a book for anyone interested in exploring the theology that underpins ministry with children and teenagers and the vision of all ages learning, living and growing in the Christian faith together. Regardless of the size of your church, the average age of your congregation, or if you have an abundance or a scarcity of resources, this book seeks to help you explore how theology can inspire and shape a growing faith for all ages in your church and community. As such, this book is for those who want to figure out how to start from scratch with children and teenagers, and for those who need to discern how to develop an already growing ministry in this area. Whether you are a churchgoer, a church leader, a children's minister, a youth pastor, a theology student, a teacher, a godparent, a parent, a church trustee, or the person who makes the coffee after church, the following chapters seek to encourage and challenge you as a disciple, as you in turn seek to belong to a church where faith and relationships grow among all ages. This book arises from our own practical experience and theological research, and we hope it connects with different denominations and traditions as it explores a treasure chest of Bible passages, theological commentary, practical ideas, tools and models to equip churches in their journey with God.[1]

Children and teenagers are important to every church and disciple. Their presence and role in the community of God's people throughout Scripture reveals their theological, missional and ministerial significance for the whole faith community. We argue that they are just as important in the health and growth of our churches today. As such, this book theologically explores and explains this importance and offers ways for churches to put this theology into practice. Chapter 1 explores key passages in Scripture describing God's relationship with children and their role and place in his kingdom on earth and in heaven. A picture begins to be formed not only of the importance of children to God, but also of their significance to adults in revealing Christ's presence and in accessing his kingdom. Chapter 2 explores the foundations of faith development theories. It draws together the work of five key thinkers, focusing particularly on the faith of young children, before offering a new way forward through the imagery of a forest. This chapter emphasizes the significance of community, imagination and openness in understanding how faith grows.

The next three chapters focus on growing faith in the context of church. Chapter 3 dives into Scripture to explore the nature of church and the presence of children and teenagers within the whole people of God – in worship, in discerning God's ways and in helping the rest of the community to inhabit God's story of salvation. This chapter identifies the significance and the hallmarks of intergenerational faith communities, both of which are further developed in Chapters 4 and 5 by rooting these findings into the life of our churches today. Chapter 4 looks at how churches can engage in intergenerational learning, proposing the key elements involved and offering ideas for how young and old can deepen their understanding of faith together. Chapter 5 explores how all generations can worship God together and grow in fellowship by sharing in the ministry of the church. It highlights the importance of our churches creating safe and encouraging spaces where children and teenagers can discern and use their gifts, and where adults can receive their ministry.

Churches, however, are not the only spaces in which children and teenagers can grow in their faith. Chapter 6 turns to look at household faith, exploring the challenges and joys of family life in the twenty-first century. It develops a theology of household faith embedded in Scripture and argues for the importance of developing community beyond the nuclear family to support growing in faith together. The chapter ends with a challenge for

## INTRODUCTION

church leaders in how they listen to families and how all these ideas might still be relevant to exploring faith with families for the very first time. Chapter 7 listens attentively to the voices of children and teenagers through empirical research carried out with over 400 children and teenagers based in schools across the north-east of England. We hear first-hand what this diverse group of children and teenagers think about God's nature and about prayer, how they read and engage with Bible stories, and the key questions with which they are wrestling. Accompanying these findings are some questions for reflection for both church and school leaders and all those involved in ministry and mission with young people across schools, households and churches.

Finally, Chapter 8 proposes that, for all ages to grow in faith together and to grow in relationship across the generations, we need to embrace change. After exploring some models of change, it offers a theology of change by observing how change is both part of the spiritual formation of disciples and part of how God guides his people ever closer to his story of salvation. A new theological and practical model is offered which seeks to mirror how we see God helping his people to navigate change throughout Scripture. This model helps churches to weave their story more tightly into Christ's ongoing story of redemption and, as such, become places where all ages can grow in faith as the generational gap is narrowed and intergenerational fellowship flourishes.

This book uncovers two important aspects of growth. One is that we grow in faith when we are part of a community of all ages. This growth in faith is about recognizing more deeply God's love for us and in turn deepening our love for God and others and letting this shape the whole of our lives. It is about more keenly anticipating God's ongoing work of transformation and strengthening our commitment to follow Christ and to revealing Christ to others. As we grow in faith, we grow in confidence in exploring, expressing and revealing our faith, and we have a surer understanding of our identity, belonging and purpose in the kingdom of heaven. We argue that this type of growth happens when all generations form and function as the body of Christ. The other type of growth is that we develop our relationships across the generations because of our faith, which helps us 'to maintain the unity of the Spirit in the bond of peace' (Eph. 4.3). When we recognize the faith that binds us together in Christ we grow in our appreciation and care of each other, in our realization of our dependence upon each other, and in our humility in receiving from each other. In other words, we grow in faith by being people of faith together. We hope this book brings inspiration to all who are praying for and seeking growth in their churches and communities, where all ages may gather and grow in faith because of the God who calls young and old to be transformed together.

## Notes

1 I (Emma) was ordained in the Church of England in 2009 and since then I have served as leader in a variety of churches. Working with children and teenagers across churches, schools and households has always been a focus of my ministry. I became the Deputy Warden at Cranmer Hall, Durham (a theological college) in 2018. During this time, I created and taught a new module on nurturing faith in children and teenagers and developed our weekly all-age worship so that we gathered as an intergenerational community where the children could serve and lead the worship. In 2024 I became the Priest in Charge in the very place where I was nurtured as a teenager.

I (Sarah) have been involved in children's and youth ministry since I was a teenager and was ordained in the Church of England in 2014. I joined the staff of Cranmer Hall in 2017 as a pastoral tutor and was appointed Dean of Anglican Formation in 2024. As part of my role, I oversee the training for children's, youth and family ministry, and my current PhD research involves conducting empirical research with children under the age of seven and their families, exploring their engagement with the Bible.

# I

# The Importance of Children and Teenagers: Digging Deeper into Theology

## EMMA L. PARKER

One of the most frequently asked questions curious children put to adults is, 'Why?' This question, which can follow conversations about death, the universe, the problem of evil or the importance of not eating earwax, can both energize and drain the saintliest of adults. However, it is precisely this question that holds immense theological significance for disciples of all ages. As we explore the importance of children and of their faith, we need to begin by asking 'Why?'[1] This book argues that children and their faith are important – and hopefully most churches would agree with this – but we need to pause, become like a child (as Jesus says[2]), and ask *Why* are children important? *Why* is their faith important? *Why* should you read this book? *Why* should we focus on children and their voices when thinking about mission, ministry and growth?

Some of us might answer by saying, 'because children are our future'. This answer comes from an honest recognition that those who are part of the church today and who are involved in its ministry are not immortal. It is an answer that is rooted in the idea that we need to 'run the race' and eventually hand over the baton to the next generation so that the church can continue. It is an answer that can stem from both fear and hope: 'I want the church to be open so I can have my funeral here,' replied a church member when we were talking about children in church. In other words, underpinning this answer is the belief that children are important in church today because they will be the adults in church in the next decade, when they can take over the mission, ministry and daily running of the church.

Hence, this seemingly innocent answer, 'because children are our future', can be embedded in the idea that children are only important because of what they can do for us in the future by plugging the gaps in church roles (and by implication, that their importance only begins when they become adults). As Margaret Withers writes, seeing children in this way is akin to us 'stocking up the freezer before heavy snow'.[3] The desire for our churches to remain open for generations to come is not in itself bad, but surely the importance of children in our churches today is not simply so that our church doors stay open tomorrow. We therefore need to dig deeper in asking and in answering, 'Why?' We must go beyond the practicalities of ensuring someone else will be the warden, the treasurer or the pastor when we step down, to understand and believe in the theological reasons why children are important in our churches now.

The reality is that many of our churches do not have children who are exploring faith, growing in their faith, or given opportunities to discern their gifts and use them to build God's kingdom here on earth. In some congregations most members are over retirement age, and many do not have children or teenagers present. Rather than ignoring our older brothers and sisters, we need to invest in how we nurture their faith and care for them when most of their world is changing. We need to ensure that our older members are given different ways in which they can still serve, so that 'in old age they still produce fruit; they are always green and full of sap' (Ps. 92.14). Alongside this however, we also need to invest in our children. This task may seem overwhelming, especially when many churches are struggling to find enough resources, whether financial, material or people; this is why we need to start with the theological question, 'Why?' As Gillian Ahlgren writes: 'When we are in darkness and confusion, theology should offer light ... Theology should empower us to integrate the wisdom of our past in order to address the urgent challenges of today.'[4] Thus, in asking why children are important, we first turn to God and listen to his Word.

## In the image of God

In Genesis we read of God saying, 'Let us make humankind in our image, according to our likeness' (1.26; see also 5.1b–2, 9.6). There have been, and still will be, many debates over what it means to be made in the image of God: is it something about how we appear, think, or feel? Is it about our spirituality or how we relate to others, or make moral decisions? Or is it to do with our purpose in the rest of creation? Perhaps Brueggemann cuts nicely across all these questions simply by stating, 'There is only one way in which God is imaged in the world and only one: humanness!'[5] Despite the complexity of understanding exactly what it means to be made in the image of God, this belief is often the theological linchpin that holds together different facets of our doctrines, our arguments around justice, and our understanding of discipleship from safeguarding to mission. Genesis 1.1–2.4 makes a theological claim 'about the character of God who is bound to his world and about the world which is bound to God'.[6] It is from this claim that the rest of the biblical story flows.

However, whether in children's Bibles or in artwork across cultures and generations, it is an image of an adult that often depicts this special scene of humankind being made in the image of God.[7] Perhaps the call to have 'dominion over', to be 'fruitful' and 'multiply' (Gen. 1.28) makes us automatically assume that God is talking about, and talking to, adults. Towner also notes about the term 'image of God' that 'although biblical scholars have explored and examined the term in depth and offered rich interpretations of it, they have rarely discussed the term in relationship to children.'[8] But in only ever picturing or talking about an adult in this scene, we might inadvertently make a theological statement about the nature of children, forgetting that they too are made in God's image and belong to this great story of creation. Hence, we must pause to consider if we sometimes treat children as if they are not yet fully human, not quite reflecting the image of God, not quite yet part of the community of humanity – possibly on the edges, but not yet fully at the centre. Perhaps this is where we need to begin, with the realization that the great theological claim in Genesis 1 includes children, for they too are a full creation of God, fully made in God's image, fully called by God and free to respond to God. As Jessy Jaison writes: 'Children are not less human than adults', for they are 'a whole person who bears this image and likeness of God and is crowned by God with glory and honor (Ps. 8:5).'[9]

Even if we have failed to imagine children as part of the great scene at the beginning of creation, we cannot fail to fully picture children as part of God's plans for peace and justice to reign in the fullness of his kingdom. In Isaiah 11.1–9 we read a prophecy that one day a new king will arise from the line of David, who will be filled with the spirit of the Lord and who will lead with righteousness and faithfulness to bring restoration and protection to the poor and vulnerable. Isaiah then pictures this reconciliation sweeping across the whole of creation, and in this scene, it is a child that takes centre stage. For in this time of restoration, predators and prey will live peacefully together: the wolf with the lamb, the leopard with the kid, the calf, the lion and the fatling, the cow and the bear. They will sleep together, eat together and nurture their young together and 'a little child shall lead them' (Isa. 11.6). It is a child who leads this 'curious assembly of animals' where the usual dividing lines of power and strength, vulnerability and weakness, have been erased.[10] Christians believe that this kingdom will be fully known across the whole of creation when Christ returns but, until then, we cling to this powerful picture of harmony with a child at the centre. A child becomes crucial in our image and understanding of the Parousia, and of the kingdom of God. It is as if God knew we might forget to picture the child at the beginning of creation, and so God has drawn for us a picture of the restoration of creation and has deliberately placed a child – as the only human being in this scene – at the centre of his future promise.

There is another biblical scene where a child is placed in the centre of a discussion which, perhaps not coincidentally, is also about power and strength, vulnerability and weakness, and the kingdom of God. This time, it is Jesus who physically places a child at the centre of the adults amid a conversation about the kingdom, and one wonders if Jesus is deliberately drawing a link to this vision in Isaiah 11. It is to this that we shall now turn.

## Children and the kingdom of heaven

In the Synoptic Gospels (Matthew, Mark and Luke) we read of a time when Jesus takes a child from the crowd and declares some amazing things about children, discipleship, entering the kingdom of heaven, and himself. Matthew's narrative of this account is the fullest (Matt. 18.1–14), with Mark and Luke separating out some elements of this narrative (Mark 9.33–37 and 42–48; Luke 9.46–48, 17.1–2 and 15.3–7). All three Gospels report that, shortly after Jesus has predicted his betrayal and death, the Disciples are discussing or even arguing over who is the greatest. In Matthew the conversation is specifically heaven-orientated: who is the 'greatest in the kingdom of heaven' (Matt. 18.1). Jesus responds with what Morna Hooker describes as an 'acted parable', for we are told that Jesus calls a child and puts the child 'among them' (Matt. 18.2), takes the child in his arms (Mark 9.36) or puts them by his side (Luke 9.47).[11] This action demonstrates Jesus' words that those who want to be first 'must be last of all and servant of all' (Mark 9.35) and that the 'least among all of you is the greatest' (Luke 9.48). Jesus is bringing a child to the centre to give a visible and tangible example of what it means to be the 'last', a 'servant' and the 'least'.

In the Greco-Roman world, children had no value for they had no economic or social status. Baby girls were left out to die.[12] Children were sold as slaves. They had no voice, no control, and could expect harsh discipline. As Miller-McLemore writes: 'The free adult male Roman citizen set the standard; children were by comparison deficient, immature, and irrational.'[13] In pointing to the child, Jesus is demonstrating what it means to be the 'least' and what it means to live as the 'last'. It is a picture filled neither with glory nor with safety. Being the last is not simply about letting someone else jump the queue; it is about an experience of life in which you have no expectations of grandeur for yourself, where you have limited choice or freedom, where others in society will seem to have an easier life with more resources. Strange writes about children that 'it was not their subjective characteristics, but their objective position in society which made them models for discipleship.'[14] In other words, to enter the kingdom, we need not seek to be the greatest but to assume an attitude of being the lowest, ready to serve, acknowledging our dependence and vulnerability.

Jesus' response in Matthew's Gospel includes more detail. Jesus first replies with a very direct ultimatum: 'unless you change and become like children, you will never enter the kingdom of heaven' (Matt. 18.3). Before the Disciples can ponder *who* is the greatest in heaven, they must consider *how* to enter heaven. It is impossible to rewind time and change our age, and we might recall Nicodemus' exclamation: 'How can anyone be born after having grown old? Can one enter a second time into the mother's womb and be born?' (John 3.4). This is in response to Jesus telling him that 'no one can see the kingdom of God without being born from above' (John 3.3). Jesus' answer in John's Gospel is that we must be born both of water and the Spirit; we must recognize and embrace our spirituality. In Matthew's Gospel, Jesus' answer is that we see the kingdom of God *in* a child and by *becoming like* a child. Matthew uses the Greek verb *strephō* (στρέφω), which here means to 'experience an inward change'.[15] Adults must change inwardly: the change is positive, it is child-shaped, and it is kingdom-orientated.

It is this inward change of becoming like a child that enables followers to fully enter the kingdom, but we are left to discern what precisely this change entails. Commentaries suggest a wide range of qualities seen in children, which adults should therefore emulate, such as trust, transparency and teachability. For Pope Francis, a young person is all about the promise of life: 'Young people have so much strength; they know how to look forward with hope. A young person is a promise of life that implies a certain degree of tenacity.'[16] As such, perhaps the inward change is for adults to become more curious, more persistently hopeful, more expectant: these characteristics would certainly help one to grow in faith and discipleship. In contrast, Gundry argues that a child belongs to the kingdom (Mark 10.14) 'without respect to their subjective attitude or activity' but because of their complete 'dependence on *God* for entering God's reign'.[17] In this case, the inward change would be about a wholehearted recognition that belonging to the kingdom is not dependent upon our works but only upon God's work of love and grace. Whether we understand this process of change to be about character or situation, Jesus himself then identifies one aspect of this internal change, for he says that humility is needed: 'Whoever becomes humble like this child is the greatest in the kingdom of heaven' (Matt. 18.4). Interestingly, humility seems to bring these two perspectives together, for humility stems from a recognition of dependence and vulnerability before God but also grows character, the fruit of which is hope.

Bonnie Thurston suggests that in pointing to a child, Jesus is saying something significant about both social status *and* character: 'The child serves as a "visual aid" of both lowliness and powerlessness as well as of the trustfulness and simplicity that deeply understands God's kingdom.'[18] However, given what Matthew reports Jesus saying next (18.5), and given our picture of the new kingdom in Isaiah 11, I would argue that Jesus is not only using a child as a visual aid, as an illustration to help the adults understand his teaching, but that the child in itself contains the 'answer' to the challenge. The child is both a signpost and the thing to which it is pointing: the child points to how one can enter the kingdom of heaven and is, in some mysterious way, the kingdom of heaven. White also tries to express this realization, proposing that children are 'the language or medium through which the kingdom of heaven is most easily and naturally conveyed' and also the revelation: 'The child standing beside Jesus, among the disciples, is the language and the revelation.'[19]

EMMA L. PARKER

## A sacred welcome

As we continue through Matthew 18, we then witness Jesus making an astonishing declaration: whoever welcomes a child in his name welcomes him (Matt. 18.5; Mark 9.37; Luke 9.48) and whoever welcomes him welcomes the one who sent him (Mark 9.37; Luke 9.48). There is an obvious relationship between the Father and the Son: in welcoming the Son, the Father is welcomed because of the Father's role in sending his Son to earth. The link here is soteriological; it is the promise made flesh. But what is the link between a child and Jesus? In welcoming children in Jesus' name, we welcome Jesus himself. The welcome is a sacred one. There is a divine link between children and Jesus and yet there is no explanation, either from the mouth of Jesus or from most theologians in the commentaries. We are left to prayerfully read this verse ourselves and make hesitant conjectures. Perhaps Jesus is pointing to the fact that he himself was born on earth as a small, vulnerable baby. God's promise for all humankind of salvation and restoration was carried in a life that was at first so small and fragile, so easily snuffed out by disease, famine or tyrannical rulers. Perhaps this miracle of the Incarnation lingers in every child's face, in every baby's cry.

Even if our understanding is limited, it is important that we, the church, take these words seriously. In welcoming children in Jesus' name, we are welcoming Jesus himself. It is a sacred welcome. Children and their faith are important because they point to the kingdom and bring Jesus into the midst of us. In the same way that Jesus called a child to stand among the adults, the child today in our church calls Jesus to stand among us all. In Isaiah 11 we have a child leading a curious assembly of animals to peace; in Matthew we have a child leading a curious assembly of adults to Jesus. We must therefore ask ourselves: what picture of a child do we have in our church? Where might we find Isaiah 11 or Matthew 18? Where is the child? In other words, where is the kingdom of heaven?

One particular day in a previous parish will always stand out in my memory. The local primary school was attending church for the mid-week service. They came once a month, and the church was full of eager children, willing and happy to take part in leading different aspects of the service. The look of joy on the children's faces to be in church was breathtaking. And yet, afterwards, there were some complaints. As the children were leaving, one person spoke loudly from the pews and told me they thought it was wrong: that I should not be letting the children come, and that children should only come to church if their parents brought them. I could see from the surprised and hurt expression on some of the children's faces that they had overheard this outburst. Hopefully my equally loud response encouraged the children and challenged these adults, but I was shocked at how far we had to travel in accepting Jesus' teaching.

We need to be intentional in how we welcome all children in Jesus' name, but also in spotting the areas in which we exclude children from encountering and revealing God, growing in their faith, and pointing to the kingdom. This would include exploring how we can welcome all children in all their diversity: the children who have different or additional learning or behavioural needs and patterns, the children who communicate using sign language, the children who have different physical or cognitive abilities and gifts, the children who carry a lot of trauma and are still navigating how to express and understand their emotions, the children who love being active and the children who love being silent. It is worth asking ourselves how we picture the scene of Jesus standing with a child in Matthew 18. Do we picture a smiling, polite, quiet child? A child tugging Jesus' sleeve and interrupting him because they want to show him their cartwheels? A child who refuses to make eye contact with the adults staring at them and who awkwardly looks at the floor? The pictures we create when reading the Bible reveal our socially set expectations and culturally shaped interpretations. An exploration of how we welcome (or exclude) children with their wide range of needs would require more time than this chapter can provide, but perhaps this is a thread you need to hold and weave into your thoughts about your church, how you serve, how you express your discipleship, how you lead, and how you pray.

Continue this conversation with others in your church. Meditate upon this passage from Matthew 18. Let it seep into you and see what changes and grows.

## Angels and mystery

In chapter 18 Matthew continues to emphasize the importance of how adults see, welcome, understand and embrace children as part of our faith community. He records Jesus' teaching that if anyone should cause one of 'these little ones' who believe in him to sin, then it would be better for them to be dead (18.6). These are strong words! The change from 'child' to 'little ones' now incorporates all those others who are the least, who are marginalized and vulnerable in society. Jesus warns his followers about making children stumble, about making them step away from the presence of God. It is clear in these verses (and those to verse 14) that Jesus and God the Father care deeply about children and their relationship with God. There is something divinely mysterious about God's relationship with children, as we see in the link that Jesus draws between welcoming a child and welcoming himself (v. 5).

For example, in verse 10 we read: 'Take care that you do not despise one of these little ones, for I tell you, in heaven their angels continually see the face of my Father in heaven.' Normally, angels must cover their eyes before God (e.g. Isa. 6.2), but these angels are allowed to look at God's face. This surely conveys something of the special nature of God's relationship with children. France notes that this is an 'expression unique in biblical literature', for there are no other occasions where we read about angels being linked to an individual.[20] These verses build a picture of children having a distinct place in God's creation, both on earth and in heaven, both in the present and in eternity. Children are not only linked with the reconciled animals in the fullness of the kingdom, but also with angels in heaven now before God's throne. Furthermore, our 'Father in heaven' desires for none of these 'little ones' to be lost, to be without him, to be away from his presence (Matt. 18.14).

It clearly took a while for the Disciples to understand the significance of Jesus' teaching, for in the next chapter Matthew records how they rebuked those who were bringing children to Jesus (19.13–15). Jesus responds by rebuking the Disciples: 'Let the little children come to me, and do not stop them; for it is to such as these that the kingdom of heaven belongs' (see also Mark 10.13–16 and Luke 18.15–17). Jesus then 'laid his hands on them' (Matt. 19.15). Gundry writes that the 'blessings of the kingdom' are given to children '*solely* on the basis of their need', and it is Jesus who takes the initiative in giving the kingdom to them.[21] It is possible that the action of laying hands on the children is not only an act of conveying blessing, but also of passing on the inheritance of the blessings of the kingdom to the children before his own death.[22]

## Conclusion

These verses raise many questions for us as a church today. They should perturb us, challenge us, inspire us and delight us. They should worry us and ignite us with hope. They should keep us awake at night and get us out of bed in the morning. Whether or not we have any responsibility of leadership in our church, we should take note of these verses for they shape discipleship for all people, shape our understanding of Jesus, and shape our vision of the kingdom. These verses point us back to our first question, 'Why?', and give us an unmistakable answer as to the importance of children and their faith. They show us in unequivocal terms that children are important to Jesus and God the Father, that they point to the kingdom and show adults how to enter the kingdom, and that they have a special and unique relationship with God through Jesus and through the angels around God's throne. Children are important because God says they are important. Children are important because adults need them to figure out how to be kingdom-orientated. Children are important because they bear the image of God and their presence ushers in the presence of Christ. Their presence is a sacred one:

in welcoming a child we welcome Christ, the king, who shows us how to become kingdom people by becoming like a child.

In all of this, there is a mysterious dance, a sacred echoing or mirroring that is being revealed in the above Bible passages. We catch a glimpse of this in the divine relationship between Christ, the child, and the eternal kingdom; the kingdom that is now and that is to come. We hear this ringing out in the belief that all are made in the image of God, and yet all who enter the kingdom need to, in some way, bear the image of a child. The child in the crowd of Disciples pointing adults to the kingdom is mirrored in the child in the crowd of animals leading creation to the final act of reconciliation. Why is the child important? Because God has declared that all children, throughout eternity, are important in his kingdom, whether on earth or in heaven. They not only reflect his image, as all women and men do, but more than this, wherever they are welcomed in Jesus' name they uniquely usher in the presence of Christ, they point to his kingdom in a way that adults do not, and they are represented in heaven around God's throne in a way that adults are not. In talking about why children are important, we tread on sacred ground, we sit around the burning bush, we kneel beside the crib and cross, we receive a basket of bread and fish, we see the gates of heaven, we feel the brush of the lion's fur and hear the bleat of the lamb – we know the voice of Christ saying, *Come*.

## Notes

1 Throughout this book I use the term 'children' to refer to teenagers as well as young children.

2 Matthew 18.3.

3 M. Withers, 2006, *Mission-Shaped Children: Moving Towards a Child-Centred Church*, London: Church House Publishing, p. ix.

4 G. T. W. Ahlgren, 2017, *The Tenderness of God: Reclaiming Our Humanity*, Minneapolis, MN: Fortress Press, p. xvi.

5 W. Brueggemann, 1982, *Genesis*, Louisville, KY: John Knox Press, p. 32.

6 Brueggemann, *Genesis*, p. 26.

7 For example, Michelangelo's *Creation of Adam*, painted in the early 1500s and which forms part of the Sistine Chapel's ceiling.

8 W. S. Towner, 2008, 'Children and the image of God', in M. J. Bunge (ed.), *The Child in the Bible*, Grand Rapids, MI: Eerdmans, pp. 307–23, p. 308.

9 J. Jaison, 2022, 'Affirming children's dignity as a theological vision and mandate', in R. Tan, N. A. Patellar and L. A. Hefford (eds), *God's Heart for Children: Practical Theology from Global Perspectives*, Carlisle, Cumbria: Langham Global Library, pp. 13–24, pp. 16, 17.

10 C. Seitz, 1993, *Isaiah 1–39: Interpretation: A Bible Commentary for Teaching and Preaching*, Louisville, KY: John Knox Press, p. 106.

11 M. D. Hooker, 1981, *The Gospel According to St Mark*, Black's New Testament Commentaries, London: Continuum, p. 228.

12 See: J. L. White, 1986, *Light from Ancient Letters*, Philadelphia, PA: Fortress Press, pp. 111–12.

13 B. J. Miller-McLemore, 2019, *Let the Children Come: Reimagining Childhood from a Christian Perspective*, Minneapolis, MN: Fortress Press, p. 80.

14 W. A. Strange, 1996, *Children in the Early Church: Children in the Ancient World, the New Testament and the Early Church*, Carlisle, Cumbria: Paternoster Press, p. 51.

15 F. W. Danker, ed., 2000, *A Greek-English Lexicon of the New Testament and other Early Christian Literature*, third edition, Chicago, IL: University of Chicago Press, p. 948.

16 Pope Francis, 2020, *A Gift of Joy and Hope*, trans. O. Stransky, London: Hodder & Stoughton, pp. 14–15.

17 J. M. Gundry, 2008, 'Children in the Gospel of Mark, with special attention to Jesus' blessing of the children (Mark 10:13–16) and the purpose of Mark', in M. J. Bunge (ed.), *The Child in the Bible*, Grand Rapids, MI: Eerdmans, pp. 143–76, pp. 152, 170.

18 B. B. Thurston, 2002, *Preaching Mark*, Minneapolis, MN: Fortress Press, p. 107.

19 K. J. White, 2008, '"He placed a little child in the midst": Jesus, the Kingdom, and Children', in M. J. Bunge (ed.), *The Child in the Bible*, Grand Rapids, MI: Eerdmans, pp. 353–74, p. 373.

20 R. T. France, 2007, *The Gospel of Matthew*, NICNT, Grand Rapids, MI: Eerdmans, p. 686.

21 Gundry, 'Children in the Gospel of Mark', p. 152.

22 Gundry, 'Children in the Gospel of Mark', p. 156.

# 2

# Exploring How Faith Grows: The Significance of Community

## SARAH STRAND

When I was talking with her, Rose (aged seven) had a very clear idea of what faith is: 'Faith is, like, believing in God.'[1] As we chatted about who God was and how she might meet him, Rose had some incredible ideas and she told me she would 'supersize' herself to see God 'because God's big'. Throughout our conversation, Rose had some key questions about the Bible as well as about her Muslim and Hindu friends from her class at school. But amid all her questions, she had a strong understanding that faith was intimately connected with belief, and specifically belief in God. What faith is, how it grows and what we can do to support (or perhaps even hinder) that growth are the key themes we will be exploring in this chapter. However, it is important to define at the outset what we mean when we're talking about faith. It is a word which seems difficult to pin down as the words faith, religion and spirituality are often used interchangeably by academics and practitioners alike. Different definitions are given depending on different disciplines, religious affiliations, individual perspectives and motivations.

When I use faith in this chapter (and indeed, in the rest of this book) it is with a distinctly Christian lens, exploring belief in the Trinitarian God: Father, Son and Holy Spirit. If we look to the Bible, Hebrews 11.1 is the clearest definition we can find: 'Now faith is the assurance of things hoped for, the conviction of things not seen.' Ronni Lamont describes faith as 'something you tease at mentally' while spirituality is about our 'deepest emotions' and how we relate to each other.[2] It is noticeable that this cognitive, knowledge-based perspective of faith is a prominent feature of a number of definitions and this presents a challenge when reflecting on faith in children, particularly the very youngest, as well as those with learning differences or disabilities.

There is sometimes a sense, particularly among some of the five key thinkers we will explore within this chapter, that a child has to attain a certain amount of knowledge to make faith a 'decision-making process'. Faith then, rather than founded in hope or in the unseen, becomes about knowledge, cognitive capacity and a 'commitment' for a child to demonstrate faith or move forward to the next stage of faith. In light of this, it's important for us to consider the faith of very young children, including babies, toddlers and pre-schoolers who are not in a position to articulate their understanding, or those children and teenagers (or adults) with additional needs who may not ever be in a position to make a formal, knowledge-based faith decision. But does this mean that they cannot or will not have faith? Absolutely not! There are, of course, developmental and cognitive elements to our understanding of theology and faith and for many of us those will be a key element of our faith. However, faith is also about those who 'receive' God and believe in him. Psalm 139.13–14 describes that 'it was you who formed my inward parts; you knit me together in my mother's womb. I praise you, for I am fearfully and wonderfully made.' A child of God is any person, created, loved and formed by God who receives him not just in knowledge (or in their heads) but in relationship (or their hearts). The Trinitarian God is a God of relationship and even the youngest or most profoundly disabled children can participate in that relationship as a foundation of their faith. The approach to faith within this book has as much to do with heart and hope as it does with head.

As we consider how to support or nurture faith in children and young people, it's important for us to understand something about how it grows, what influences and shapes it and what the key markers of faith are. This chapter particularly focuses on the faith of young children as a key foundation for what will come next as faith grows and changes. We will explore the faith development models of James Fowler, John Westerhoff, Heinz Streib, Tobin Hart and Sarah Brush before I offer my own picture of faith development.

## Models of faith development

### Fowler's stages of faith

James Fowler, heavily influenced by developmental psychologists Jean Piaget,[3] Lawrence Kohlberg and Erik Erikson, sought to provide a developmental framework for faith, which he defines as a three-way relationship between:

1. a person (and the way they experience themselves, others and the world)
2. what they believe about what is important in life
3. the way they shape their life purpose and meaning

Fowler argues that faith is an integral part of the development of a person's character and personality and the development of faith is driven by images and 'constructions' in a person's life.[4] Fowler divides faith development into six stages, with an earlier stage of 'Infancy and Undifferentiated Faith' which is not given a stage number. The stages are sequential:

Stage 1: Intuitive-Projective Faith (ages 2–7)
Stage 2: Mythic-Literal Faith (ages 7–12)
Stage 3: Synthetic-Conventional Faith (ages 13–18+)
Stage 4: Individuative-Reflective Faith (ages 20–40)
Stage 5: Conjunctive Faith (ages 40–80)
Stage 6: Universalizing Faith (adulthood, but extremely rare)

Fowler emphasizes throughout his work that, while the stages correspond with ages throughout childhood, adolescence and adulthood, it is possible for adults to inhabit any of the stages. This point is illustrated with numerous interviews with adults Fowler perceives to be in the early stages of faith development.

Fowler's goal with producing the stages of faith is to 'enhance' an individual's progression between life phases to bring new and enriching ways of 'being in faith'.[5] Fowler is careful to outline that his understanding of 'faith' is not restricted to a particular religion or worldview; rather he sees faith as a key aspect of being human. Therefore, for Fowler, attending to the development of faith enables a person to progress to a new phase of life, leaving the markers of the previous phase behind. Fowler clearly points out that the stages of faith are not a set of achievements to be ticked off (as in the case of a much-desired swimming certificate), nor are they goals to aim for, they are rather to illustrate the 'time, experience, challenge and nurture ... required for growth in faith'.[6] Fowler uses them to identify which stage he perceives someone to be at in their life of faith. Through his model, Fowler has linked psychosocial theories of human development with faith development, with the goal of unity between the two (in an ideal circumstance) or remedying differences in stages, as key to human flourishing.

With each of the key thinkers within this chapter, we will explore the first stage of faith development. The reasons for this are twofold: firstly because under sevens are the least well researched age bracket when it comes to children's faith and secondly because these first stages are seen as foundational for the stages which come afterwards and therefore understanding more about the first phase is significant for reflecting more broadly on faith nurture among children and young people.

*Stage 1: Intuitive-projective faith*

Within this stage, Fowler argues that children cannot 'coordinate and compare two different perspectives on the same object'.[7] He also maintains Piaget's understanding of young children as egocentric, arguing that conversation with children in this age bracket often takes the form of a monologue as children can struggle to coordinate their perspective with that of another person. This developmental assumption has been increasingly challenged over the last few decades and it risks creating stereotypes of young children who can often be very empathetic.

*Stories, images and magic*

Fowler describes the thought of children within Stage 1 as 'fluid and magical' as he perceives they have not yet been stifled by 'stable logical operations'.[8] He also recognizes the significance of stories and images for children in Stage 1. The key stories and images in a child's life are often formed by the surrounding culture they live in but are also strongly influenced by family. Stories and images are a key way of children developing their own pictures and understanding of God or the sacred, which is why it is important to consider the storytelling landscape children have.[9] What are the key images of God they are offered (is it a God who is loving and kind?), is that facilitated by images from picture books or stories? And which stories are read? These images of God are not just formed by the Bible stories they read, but by the other stories they encounter in all different forms as they discover more about the world around them.

*The power of imagination*

A key aspect of storytelling and imagery for children is imagination. And imagination is an important aspect of development in Stage 1, particularly as it has a powerful impact on future faith development. This is important to notice, particularly when it comes to enabling and empowering children in play, which is so significant for a child's overall well-being and development. However, imagination can be powerful both in positive and constructive ways but also in potentially destructive ways. If a child's imagination is exposed to unrestrained images of destruction and terror this can have a profound negative impact on faith development. Fowler connects this particularly to ways of reinforcing taboos, doctrines and morality within a child's life.[10] This highlights the need for substantial attention to be paid to the quality and content of images children are given. It also points to the importance for children of establishing trusting relationships with adults and carers to create an environment in which the child can express images he or she is forming. Developing 'faith-talk' as a regular practice can be a helpful practice here which enables adults to offer appropriate support when destructive images have been formed. A child I know had seen a particularly gruesome depiction of Jesus' crucifixion which had led to (among other things!) a fear of communion wine as they associated it with drinking blood. Enabling the child to explore the fears and concerns which arose with a trusted adult was key in listening to, supporting and reframing the scary image the child had been left with.

This emphasizes again the reality that primary carers (in the early years I would argue this includes parents but also grandparents, key workers in nursery or education settings and close family friends) are the most significant influence on a child's faith and development in this stage. Children will rely heavily on imitating, or copying, what they see in adults around them. The example set by primary carers in faith practices, in storytelling, in faith-talk and in the visible and ritualized aspects of faith are hugely influential on the child's developing faith landscape.

*Progression to Stage 2*

There are important insights and strengths within Fowler's work on Stage 1 to equip and enable parents and those who care for children to understand the ways in which a child *might* be developing in faith and to support that development. However, Fowler's goal of supporting the child through to enable them to reach Stage 2 is problematic. He writes that the main factor precipitating that transition is 'the emergence of concrete operational thinking' and the growing concern is to distinguish 'between what is real and what only seems to be'.[11] It is not clear exactly what Fowler means in the distinction between what is real and what isn't, but his line of argument suggests that the realm of the magical, imaginative, story-filled, image-rich world should be left behind for progression to the concrete and real. While a previous stage is incorporated into the landscape of a new stage, there is substantial loss here for the adult or child who is led to believe that discerning between 'real' and 'not real' is what is required. There is little space here for the work of the Holy Spirit or for the ongoing significance of imagination and play in the faith-lives of both children and adults.

## Westerhoff's stages of faith

John Westerhoff is a key thinker in the field of Christian Education who argues for the importance of socialization and relationships alongside formal schooling (whether in public education or discipleship within the church) in his approach to Christian Education. In his significant work *Will Our Children Have Faith?*, Westerhoff sought to clarify what he perceives to be the goal of discipleship or, to use his word, catechesis as 'to form Christ-like communal persons and communities. This implies for me a clarity of *faith*, of how we are to perceive God.'[12] Building upon the foundation of Fowler's work, Westerhoff sought to develop his own stages of faith as a means of first understanding and then expanding faith through Christian catechesis. In an important distinction from Fowler however, Westerhoff writes from a solely Christian perspective amid a well-developed understanding of the faith community as connected with the body of Christ. Faith, from Westerhoff's definition is 'understood as a way of behaving',[13] which can be described in generalized terms but always in the context of Christian community. Westerhoff's stages are as follows:

Stage 1 – Experienced Faith
Stage 2 – Affiliative Faith
Stage 3 – Searching Faith
Stage 4 – Owned Faith

To explore his stages, Westerhoff uses the analogy of rings in a tree trunk – each stage in the development of a tree is complete and whole but it is expanding all the time. In a departure from Fowler, there is no hierarchy within the stages and Westerhoff argues that the goal of expanding into new styles of faith is 'not so as to possess better or greater faith, but only to fulfil one's faith potential'.[14] This potential is outlined as an individual playing their part in a Christ-like community. While Westerhoff argues otherwise, there is a clear sense of hierarchy within the ascending numbers of the stages as well as within the developmental and age connections made – which, in turn, connect with the influence of Piaget and Fowler. Again, it is problematic that young children are always placed in the first stage of any developmental sequence, which communicates an underlying assumption that the stage is undesirable as progression from it (even for adults) is necessary for both human and spiritual flourishing.

## Stage 1 – Experienced faith

Westerhoff identifies the preschool and childhood years as the location for experienced faith, characterized by enactive experience. Westerhoff notes: 'The child explores and tests, imagines and creates, observes and copies, experiences and reacts.'[15] Again, picking up on similar themes to Fowler, he recognizes the mirror children often are to the key carers around them. Westerhoff also makes a powerful connection between the importance of a consistent connection between language and experience. For example, if a child is repeatedly told of God's love, kindness and compassion but simultaneously experiences abuse, neglect and harsh punishment they will understandably find it difficult to connect feelings of happiness and security with their image, language and understanding of God. While it may seem like an obvious thing to say, the significance of parental and key caregiving relationships cannot be underestimated in the early years of a child's life and this remains true across all aspects. Attending to and nurturing parental faith is therefore enormously significant for enabling the faith growth of children and young people.

Westerhoff's ultimate point is that enculturation is the means of Christian education[16] and therefore paying close attention to the particular ways culture and experience are shaping an individual child's development forms an important part of this process. Children are rooted within specific family contexts, alongside other key influences of culture including (but not limited to) church and school. What images of God are they receiving in each of these contexts? If they attend a church school, for example, how are the school values shaping their understanding of the nature of God?[17] What images of God are most prominent in their church culture (e.g. an emphasis on the ministry of the Holy Spirit or on the crucifixion)? Even if a child does not have any obvious 'faith' cultures, they are continually shaped by the other images which are most prioritized within their culture and context. Faith for Westerhoff is deeply rooted in the everyday reality of Christian community and family culture and this is an important theme which we will explore more deeply in Chapter 6.

## Streib's styles of religion

Heinz Streib's Styles of Religion mark a move away from a focus on cognition or knowledge within faith development theories.[18] The language he uses emphasizes *religion* rather than faith and he offers criticism on Fowler's 'Faith Stages' without acknowledging (or explaining) his own use of different terminology. It is also important to note that he is also working from within a different psychological approach to Piaget. Within his styles, Streib recognizes the importance of four 'dimensions' to the development of religion which he describes as the psychodynamic-interpersonal dimension, the relational-interpersonal dimension, the interpretive-hermeneutic dimension and the life-world dimension.[19] Within these dimensions Streib identifies religious development as a complex set of interrelated factors between the relationships (schemata) and experiences (themata) in a person's life history which change over the course of a lifetime and are shaped by variations in personal, social and societal relationships.[20] Streib's five styles are as follows:

1. Subjective-Religious Style
2. Instrumental-Reciprocal Religious Style
3. Mutual Religious Style
4. Individuative-Systemic Religious Style
5. Dialogical Religious Style

The purpose of Streib's styles is to identify the rituals, symbols and narratives that relate to a person's life history and contribute to the transformation and development of religion over the course of a lifetime, which also inform and correspond to a person's relationships.[21] Streib produced his stages in the 'milestone model'. The model illustrates peaks and troughs, with a culminating peak in each style while the previous style continues to exist on a lower level. This model enables flexibility with the time and age-bracket restrictions of other theories while recognizing the ongoing integration and relevance of a style after it has peaked.[22] There is still a distinct hierarchical development in Streib's styles, as with Fowler and Westerhoff, but it allows for a slightly more complex picture of growth and development in contrast to Westerhoff's image of concentric circles.

Streib gives age indicators on both the first two stages, describing the Subjective-Religious Style as incorporating 'early childhood',[23] while noting that the Instrumental-Reciprocal Style corresponds with Fowler's mythic-literal faith which incorporates children aged 7–12. Streib, while pushing against the influence of cognitive developmental theory nonetheless draws upon the age categorizations for his own work, which is significant: while he aims to broaden the landscape of faith development theory, he recognizes the importance of the first two age brackets in particular for the growth of faith in children under 12.

## Subjective-religious style

Streib draws upon the language of Piaget and Fowler to describe the attributes of young children (aged 2–7) in this style. He identifies the mirroring and egocentricity of this phase while also recognizing that an important outcome for this age bracket is the development of trust, facilitated by healthy adult relationships. Streib also emphasizes the significance of fantasy, images and feelings[24] in this phase, which are shared characteristics with all the early phases of development we have already explored.

The differences between Streib's work and the early phases in Piaget, Fowler and Westerhoff are minimal – with the important distinction of the milestone model, which offers a more complex overall structure. A strength of Streib's work is his emphasis on the importance of life narrative within faith development. An individual incorporates material from their life to develop a story that, in turn, integrates and retells stories from earlier styles and stages.[25] Storytelling, both of a person's own story, as well as the stories they hear, read and absorb throughout their lives, is hugely influential on their faith journey. This is something again to take note of and it is helpful to reflect on the stories (in a range of formats and different media) children and young people absorb. This is not to take a restrictive approach but one of curiosity; what stories are shaping their understandings of the world, of other people and themselves? Do those stories contrast with the biblical story or complement it? Where is the space for complexity, for challenge and for listening to children and young people tell their own stories of faith?

There are striking similarities across all different models, stages and styles of developmental faith theories in the earliest phases. It is interesting to explore the reasons behind this: one might be the challenge of research with younger children, both ethically and practically.[26] It is also difficult for children to articulate their concepts of faith and religion when their language capabilities may prevent this, or, more accurately, might prevent adults from understanding their unique perspectives. The divergent motivations and perspectives behind each model of faith development are also significant, with an emphasis placed on children (or adults new to faith) progressing through a hierarchy towards a developed, adult faith in some form. It is also important to acknowledge that there are core ideas and understandings that seem both common and unique to children in these phases and which offer helpful insight into how children learn and engage with faith and religion – although it is clear much deeper testing or exploration of these theories with young children is needed.

While the approaches of Piaget, Fowler, Westerhoff and Streib differ, there seems to be consensus that significant things happen as children develop cognitively, socially and culturally (among other aspects) through that period of life.

## Hart – five styles

In *The Secret Spiritual World of Children*, Tobin Hart seeks to illuminate, explore, explain and support the inner spiritual lives of children. His approach, founded in an entirely different psychological perspective to Piaget, reacts against the restrictions of the cognitive-developmental approach which has characterized the other voices in this chapter so far. Hart places the language of spirituality at the heart of his pursuit, taking pains to separate it from religion or knowledge-based faith development. Hart takes a broad approach to his sources of spiritual wisdom, frequently citing texts from across the major global religions and mystic sources. Interestingly, while he draws upon the mystic Christian tradition heavily, he rarely acknowledges or engages with the Bible. In one of only a handful of references, Hart seeks to argue that Jesus was advocating for belief in reincarnation in Matthew 17.10–13 which is undoubtedly problematic from a Christian theological perspective.[27]

Hart's understanding of Christian theology is misguided at best and he is wary of any research into 'God talk' in relation to how children think and talk relating to a particular religious doctrine. You might wonder, therefore, why he is included within this chapter! What is interesting in Hart's approach is that he prioritizes the significance of spiritual experience over logical thought and linguistic capacity in children. Hart believes doctrinal frameworks will squash a child's spiritual life, which I would argue is a step too far in the opposite direction of what the developmental faith theories are seeking to offer. However, it is significant to notice that while Fowler and Westerhoff leave limited capacity for spiritual engagement within their models, Hart (while having dismissed cognitive developmental theory and offered substantial criticism of it) still cannot escape from drawing upon it as he seeks to assist parents and caregivers to nurture spirituality. He discusses children's 'distinctly unwise, naïve, impulsive and self-indulgent' characteristics as well as expressing that

> while children may be expressing profundities of the wisest adults in one moment, they may be emotionally like a four-year-old when it comes to sharing toys, like a ten-year-old in relationships with friends, and like a thirteen-year-old when it comes to the self-discipline required to finish their homework.[28]

Piaget's influence (as much as Hart wishes to escape it) is clear here and even Hart recognizes there are distinct developmental issues which are pertinent to different age groups of children.

Hart offers his own five styles through which he seeks to identify the 'spiritual temperament' of a child, 'the style ... through which the child's spirituality most naturally flows':[29]

1 Wisdom
2 Wonder
3 Wondering
4 The Meeting Between You and Me
5 Seeing the invisible

Hart does not attach a particular age bracket or developmental stage to his styles, in contrast with Fowler, Westerhoff and Streib. His main goal through identifying these styles seems to be to enable parents (and through them, children) to understand and nurture these aspects of spiritual temperament. Hart is at pains to accuse religious thinkers of separating the spiritual and religious while at the same time wanting to remove the influence of religious doctrine from a child's spirituality. While he offers many helpful checks to the trend towards prioritizing cognitive engagement, his dismissal of the benefits of religious and doctrinal frameworks is short-sighted and results in the construction of his own 'spiritual curriculum' to bridge the gap that dismissal creates. Hart opened the conversation about children's spirituality which has continued through the work of Rebecca Nye,[30] among others, and in the children's spirituality movement that has flourished over the last two decades as research and understanding in this area has increased dramatically. However, developmental thinkers have had a lasting influence on our understanding of children, the landscape of their faith and inner spiritual life. It is important that this understanding is balanced by discussions around faith, religion and spirituality in childhood which recognize the value of understanding the child as a whole person. So how can we move forward with a more integrated approach to faith and spirituality with that in mind?

## Sarah Brush's tree

Sarah Brush offers one possible way forward, building upon Westerhoff's imagery of the rings of a tree trunk and developing her own model based on the life cycle of a tree. Explored within Ronni Lamont's *Faith in Children*, Brush's model establishes the stages of the life cycle of a tree from seed to sapling, sapling to maturity, to *totum*.[31] Brush emphasizes the need for the careful nurturing of saplings, or those who are young in the faith, and uses the image of staking trees in the act of offering security and strength as children are nurtured and grow in faith. Brush's stages take into consideration the conditions above and below the ground – the need for fertile soil as well as the impact of the seasons. She also strikingly explores the image of the *totum*, a tree which is dying but still harbours plentiful life and offers refuge for other living creatures. Brush hasn't developed this image further and it is distinctive from the four developmental thinkers we have already engaged with as it is based not in developmental psychology but rather in imagery and metaphor. I think that is perhaps one of the most helpful things about it. Brush has only this year written extensively on the underlying theological perspectives of the tree image in her new book *The Way Through The Trees* (2025) and I would like to build on it further by offering the image of the forest of faith as perhaps a way forward for exploring models of faith nurture and growth.

## *The forest of faith*

I sat on the front terrace of Shepherd's Dene Retreat House in Northumberland, while in the middle of leading a retreat, praying and reflecting on the themes of faith and vocation we were using as a focus for the weekend. Shepherd's Dene has the most beautiful view down a valley, with gardens and woodland in the immediate foreground and the rolling hills of Northumberland in the distance. It was the beginning of November, so there was dew on the ground, a chill in the air and a beautiful combination of trees which were in different stages of progressing into the dormancy autumn and winter bring. Some evergreen trees were standing bold, tall and stark on the skyline, next to trees of different sizes which had shed their leaves and the shrubs and plants of the foreground. The scene was so diverse, with the most incredible combination of greens, browns, blues and greys and it led me to reflect on a model of faith development which is not about an individual tree, or a hierarchy of progressing through different stages but as a diverse forest – recognizing the beauty of shared life and the reality of everyday faith.

## *Roots*

The Bible is full of organic imagery which explores seeds, plants and trees. In fact, 'the Bible mentions trees more than it mentions any living thing besides humans.'[32] There are many occasions, however, where trees and people are mentioned alongside one another or when the image of a tree is used to describe a person's faith. Psalm 1.1–3 describes a person who delights and meditates on the law of the Lord as 'like a tree planted by streams of water, which yields its fruit in season and whose leaf does not wither' (NIV). The image here is about God's law, contained within the overarching narrative of the Bible, providing the living water which nurtures the tree (or the person) to grow and produce fruit. There are very similar echoes in Jeremiah 17.7–8 in which the person who puts their trust and confidence in the Lord 'will be like a tree planted by the water that sends out its roots by the stream. It does not fear when heat comes; its leaves are always green. It has no worries in a year of drought and never fails to bear fruit.' The connection this time is made to trust and confidence, drawing on a relationship with God which offers sustenance and growth but also protection from the elements. This imagery is picked up again in Psalm 92.12–15 when the 'righteous will flourish like a palm tree ... planted in the house of the LORD' (NIV).

There are also echoes throughout the Gospels and particularly in the parables Jesus told here, including Mark 4.3–9 in which the Word of God is sown and falls on different soil, yielding different outcomes. Jesus often used tree or plant-based images and parables to explore faith, fruitfulness or prepare his disciples for his return (Matt. 13.1–9, 18–23, 31–32; Mark 4.26–29). Jesus also describes himself as the True Vine (John 15.1–17), identifying the connection of his followers to the vine as 'branches'.

The connecting image here for faith development is about roots: both where they are planted and what is sustaining them. For faith to flourish it needs roots which access living water (Jesus). Trees are able to grow and establish in many surprising places but their root structure needs to be strong and they need to find food from somewhere. Have you ever seen a tree growing out of the centre of a rock? Or on the side of a cliff? Often it seems those trees defy probability, but they can have a very long tap root winding through inside the crevices of the rock into a place of long-hidden nourishment. As we engage in our own journeys of faith, and support children and young people with theirs, I wonder if we are able to identify where their roots are? Are they freshly established and vulnerable? Are they deep and nourishing? Are they growing in seemingly impossible ground but still holding on? And what is the nourishment they are receiving? Do they have space and opportunity to encounter Bible stories, images of God, use their imaginations, play and wonder? Are they 'planted in the house of the Lord' and have they been empowered to talk about God and faith, engage in the rituals of their community and question them?

Within the forest of faith there are many possibilities here. There are small trees with mighty root systems and there are enormous oaks with deep, strong foundations which are uprooted in the harshest winter storm. The roots are below the surface and therefore not always easy to see, but they are always growing, changing and seeking out nourishment. And while trees endure the seasons and things change, through periods of dormancy and challenge and factors beyond their own choosing, when food and water are hard to find their roots hold them (however unsteadily) in the ground. Which leads to the next set of questions: what season are the children and teenagers we know and love in right now? Are they being battered in a storm? Are their roots under strain? Are they flourishing after a long period with little nourishment? And how can we support them as they navigate the season they are in right now?

*The forest ecosystem*

A forest (generally) contains a combination of different trees and plants at different stages of growth and development. Each individual tree contributes something unique and important (as well as beautiful) to the flourishing of the whole. Research has been conducted which shows that trees within a forest are connected by both their roots and the fungi of the soil and they are able to communicate with each other, share nutrients and resources and even pass on when defences are needed to promote the health of the whole ecosystem. Faith does not happen, or grow, in isolation but as part of a whole community. These images of faith development, and their accompanying questions, are not just for children and young people but for adults too as faith changes and grows through all ages and life stages. Trees need roots but they also need community – other trees, shrubs, birds and wildlife as well as sources of water and food – in order to not just survive but thrive. Sarah Brush refers to the need to 'stake' young saplings in order to flourish, which describes the ministry of faith nurture or 'growing faith' in children and young people.[33] But that process seems to not recognize the roots which are trying to establish or any of the other elements which may impact or influence the growing sapling.

I wonder if it would be more fruitful to recognize the work of the ecosystem, or the community, as a whole and the reality of growing in faith together. Trees gain strength as they are exposed to the elements and as a consequence their roots respond by strengthening. But they are also nurtured and protected by the trees which surround them. Saplings grow under the protection of bigger trees; the space created by fallen trees enables new trees to grow and they are connected through a beautiful and complex diversity. No tree is at the same stage, every tree is unique although there may be markers we can identify across trees of a certain age; as identified in the key themes we can see through the work of Fowler, Westerhoff, Streib and Hart. Each tree is affected differently by its particular positioning, soil quality and the elements around it. This calls us to recognize the uniqueness of each child and teenager. Even those who grow up in the same household will have different experiences and will be rooted in different places. Children and teenagers (and adults!) need to be deeply known and deeply loved and the best place for that is in community, both in their own households but also within the body of Christ. Without wanting to mix too many metaphors, the forest ecosystem is the body of Christ and faith grows and is nurtured in an environment in which each individual person can be acknowledged and recognized.

And in the end, we are talking about humans and not trees! But I hope the image is helpful in enabling us to place a much deeper emphasis on exploring roots but also on relationship building, listening and community as we move towards growing together in faith as both adults and children. The forest faith image I hope to see in the life of the church is one of diversity and complexity which reflects the messy and challenging but also beautiful and joyful journey of faith across a lifetime.

## Conclusion

In this chapter we have explored some of the key voices and methods of recognizing faith development in younger children, as well as my own proposal of the image of a forest in enabling us to explore faith across all ages. There isn't a simple means of measuring a child against a particular stage of faith and doing so, as I highlighted at the beginning of this chapter, restricts those whose faith is not based on knowledge. As we seek to grow together in faith *with* children and teenagers however, there are some key themes which have consistently emerged: the significance of close, caring relationships marked by trust; the importance of imagination, play and magic in young lives; recognizing the unique identity of each child, attending to their storytelling and spiritual landscapes; making space for their relationship with God; and finally, the essential component of community faith.

### Notes

1 This conversation happened as part of my PhD empirical research. Rose's name has been changed and our interview was conducted with full ethical approval from the University of Aberdeen.
2 Ronni Lamont, 2020, *Faith in Children*, Oxford: Lion Hudson, p. 77.
3 Jean Piaget, 1951, *The Child's Conception of the World*, London: Routledge.
4 James Fowler, 1981, *Stages of Faith: The Psychology of Human Development and the Quest for Meaning*, New York: HarperOne, p. 92.
5 Fowler, *Stages of Faith*, p. 114.
6 Fowler, *Stages of Faith*, p. 114.

7 Fowler, *Stages of Faith*, p. 123.
8 Fowler, *Stages of Faith*, p. 123.
9 Fowler, *Stages of Faith*, p. 128.
10 Fowler, *Stages of Faith*, p. 133–4.
11 Fowler, *Stages of Faith*, p. 134.
12 John Westerhoff, 2012, *Will our Children have Faith?*, third edition, New York: Morehouse Publishing, p. 47.
13 Westerhoff, *Will our Children have Faith?*, p. 90.
14 Westerhoff, *Will our Children have Faith?*, p. 90.
15 Westerhoff, *Will our Children have Faith?*, p. 92.
16 Westerhoff, *Will our Children have Faith?*, p. 99.
17 The research explored in Chapter 7 would suggest that this often happens in very significant ways.
18 Heinz Streib, 'Faith development theory revisited: the religious styles perspective', *International Journal for the Psychology of Religion*, 11 3 (2001), pp. 143–58.
19 Streib, 'Faith development theory revisited', p. 144.
20 Streib, 'Faith development theory revisited', p. 146.
21 Streib, 'Faith development theory revisited', p. 149.
22 Streib, 'Faith development theory revisited', p. 149.
23 Streib, 'Faith development theory revisited', p. 150.
24 Streib, 'Faith development theory revisited', p. 150.
25 Streib, 'Faith development theory revisited', p. 148.
26 Piaget identified that laboratory testing was only possible once a child reached the age of four. Piaget, *The Child's Conception of the World*, p. 35.
27 Tobin Hart, 2003, *The Secret Spiritual World of Children*, Makawao, HI: Inner Ocean, p. 141.
28 Hart, *The Secret Spiritual World of Children*, p. 217.
29 Hart, *The Secret Spiritual World of Children*, p. 10.
30 Rebecca Nye, 2009, *Children's Spirituality: What It Is and Why It Matters*, London: Church House Publishing.
31 Lamont, *Faith in Children*, p. 89.
32 Kevin Hargaden and Ciara Murphy, 2022, *The Parish as Oasis: An Introduction to Practical Environmental Care*, Dublin: Messenger Publications, p. 92.
33 Lamont, *Faith in Children*, p. 89.

# 3

# The Whole People of God: Old and New Testament Insights

## EMMA L. PARKER

Over the last few decades a wide range of research projects and papers have been commissioned to explore factors contributing to the nurture of children's faith.[1] One such paper was published in 2019 and has been, possibly more than any other, a catalyst to awaken more and more people to consider their approach to nurturing the faith of children and teenagers. 'Growing Faith' was published by the Church of England to set out a vision for churches, schools and households to intentionally work together to create the kind of relationships and opportunities needed for faith to grow. The summary states:

> *Growing Faith* envisions children, young people and households coming to faith, growing in discipleship and contributing confidently to the Kingdom of God through the community of faith. It is about how, as members of the whole people of God, children and young people are encouraged and how the whole Church is equipped to think intergenerationally.[2]

It questions whether the church is 'sufficiently focused' on engaging with children and young people, and argues that the church needs to develop how it enables and empowers children's faith to grow and thrive.[3] This chapter and the following two will focus on the relationship between the church and the child, by first exploring the nature of the church and how we see children participating in the gatherings of God's people through Scripture. This will then help us in Chapters 4 and 5 to explore how today's church can be an intergenerational faith community, where children are not only welcomed, but where their faith is treasured, nurtured and active in growing the kingdom for the benefit of all ages.

## The nature of church: belonging and fellowship

The New Testament uses the Greek word *ekklēsia* to refer to the assembly or gathering of people who are united together by a common belief and participation in Jesus Christ as Lord. The word *ekklēsia* is often translated as 'church', but rather than it being used to refer to a specific building where people gather, it points to a specific group of people who form the 'household of God' on earth, which is 'built upon the foundation of the apostles and prophets, with Christ Jesus himself as the cornerstone' (Eph. 2.19–20). There may be different denominations, expressions and local gatherings of church, but they are all considered to belong to each other as one for they all belong to its head, Jesus Christ (Col. 1.18, 2.19; Eph. 1.22, 4.15). This church, which is for those from every nation and race, is therefore 'the sphere in which hostility has been overcome, reconciliation has been achieved, and peace bears its fruits, and, as such, forms a visible sign of unity for the world'.[4]

The Apostles' Creed thus describes it as the 'holy catholic church'.[5] It is 'catholic' in the sense that it is 'whole', with its members held together by baptism into Christ through the Spirit (1 Cor. 12.13) and united 'in Christ' with all their differences in gender, social or economic status, and ethnicity (Gal. 3.28). The church is fundamentally connected to Christ, and is often described as the one body of Christ (e.g. 1 Cor. 12.12–31; Col. 3.14–16; Eph. 1.20–23, 4.12; see also 'one body *in* Christ', Rom. 12.4–5) where the different members work together to promote 'the body's growth in building itself up in love' (Eph. 4.16). This image also points out the important 'notion that we have responsibilities to and for one another'.[6] In other words, the church is not a place we visit for an hour each week sitting at arm's length in our pews, but a living body which has daily needs and roles with the aim of growing in love. As a body, Bonhoeffer therefore argues that, 'Christ's place on earth has been taken by his Body, the Church. The Church is the real presence of Christ.'[7] The church is therefore the church *of* God: while it is found in specific geographic areas through time, it primarily belongs to the eternal God.[8] The identity and continuing life of the church is not so much connected to a geographical place as it is to God himself: it is *of* God, found *in* God and the Lord Jesus Christ (1 Thess. 1.1).

Hence, an important feature of the church is its *koinōnia* with God, which means participating and sharing in something of God and his acts of redemption. Paul reminds the Corinthian church that they came into being through the faithfulness of God, for they were 'called into the fellowship of his Son, Jesus Christ our Lord' (1 Cor. 1.9), where for Paul, fellowship with Christ is about sharing in the fruit of Christ's death and resurrection (Phil. 3.10; see also 1 Cor. 10.16). The church's fellowship with God is not only Christocentric, but also Spirit-orientated, for disciples have 'fellowship of the Spirit' (Phil. 2.1), which, rather than meaning togetherness, refers to 'a *partnership* of common interest, forged and empowered by the Holy Spirit'.[9] As such, churches today often use the blessing-prayer found in 2 Corinthians 13.13 at the end of their worship or prayer meetings, which hopes for the fellowship of the Holy Spirit to be with all their members. Nick and Becky Drake point to the work of the Spirit in enabling fellowship to happen within the body of Christ between its members (Rom. 8.14–16): 'It is the shared presence of the Spirit of God that makes our participation in the big family of God possible.'[10]

In the New Testament this fellowship with God spills over into fellowship with all members of the church, evidenced in different ways. Whereas the word 'fellowship' in the contemporary church is often used synonymously with 'friendship', a more accurate meaning is of *participation* and *sharing* in something common with other members in the body. Other verses using *koinōnia* show that it is about how believers share their gifts to care for each other, share ministry with other members, and share in worship together. For example, some members from the churches in Macedonia and Achaia have delighted in sharing their belongings with others in the Jerusalem church who are in need (Rom. 15.26; see also 2 Cor. 8.4, 9.13), and Paul reports that he and Barnabas were given the 'right hand of fellowship' by James, Cephas and John who agreed that Paul and Barnabas should preach to the Gentiles while they preached to the 'circumcised' (Gal. 2.9). Receiving fellowship meant that the calling of Paul and Barnabas was recognized by other members of the church, and that the church supported the sharing out of mission and ministry. Finally, in Acts we read that the new believers were devoting themselves 'to the apostles' teaching and fellowship, to the breaking of bread and the prayers' (2.42). It is likely that the latter two activities were given to define what *koinōnia* looked like for these believers.[11]

Thus, *koinōnia* with God and with other members can neither be separated from each other nor from our understanding of *ekklēsia*.[12] The simple practice of sharing becomes a sacred practice of fellowship, rooted in the generosity of God, through the acts of Christ, made possible by the power of the Spirit. This type of sacred sharing may result in the type of friendship we often understand by the word 'fellowship', in what Bonhoeffer calls a 'visible fellowship' where the 'physical presence of other Christians is a source of incomparable joy and strength to the believer'.[13] Thus, when Paul urges believers to love one another (and those outside the church) with abundance (e.g. 1 Thess. 3.12; Rom. 12.10; Col. 3.14), to do good to one another (e.g. 1 Thess. 5.15; Gal. 6.10) and to share their goods with those in need (1 Tim. 6.18), these are practical outworkings of a sharing that goes beyond mere acquaintanceship to a kinship that stems from the divine. For through Christ alone 'do we have access to one another, joy in one another, and fellowship with one another'.[14]

## Summary

The church is a group of people united not just by their common belief in Jesus as Lord, but called and brought together by God so that all members have fellowship with Christ and the Spirit, and with each other. The church is both local and specific, rooted in a geographical context, but also universal and eternal, rooted in Christ. A vital part of the church is the fellowship that each member can experience: fellowship of a divine nature whereby we share in the death and resurrection of Christ, and fellowship of a human nature whereby we participate in a sacred sharing of care, ministry, calling, worship and resources for the growth of the whole body.

This brief exploration of the nature of church raises some key questions for thinking about children and the church: How can church be a place where children are seen to be true members of the body of Christ, with a purpose and a role that serves the whole body? How can church be a place where children discover how we can gather with all our beautiful differences and find unity and belonging within our diversity? How can children participate and share in the divine and earthly *koinōnia*? We need to seriously and persistently ask if, in our understanding of church, we have included or excluded children. In a commentary exploring Ephesians, the author writes some inspiring reflections after his exegesis on Ephesians 2.11–22, including the following:

> The Church is where men and women experience a sense of being at home, of belonging, not only to one another in a unified humanity as fellow citizens, but also to God himself as part of his household or family.[15]

This is a beautiful summary of Paul's vision for the church. However, one thing is missing: where are the children and teenagers? Is this church not also a place where children can be at home, find belonging, unity and God? We will return to some of these questions in the next two chapters, but for now we will turn to look at how children have been part of God gathering his people throughout the Old Testament and the New Testament, and how they have partnered with God.

## The whole people of God: travelling through Scripture

In Chapter 1 we explored the importance of children in God's eyes. It comes as no surprise then to find that children are present at significant gatherings and events in the developing story of God's people, and that they also play a significant part in this story. Children were part of the covenantal relationship as much as the adults: not only should they know that the Lord alone was their God, but also that they were to show absolute faithfulness to God. The Old Testament scholar, Walter Brueggemann, notes that important in the covenantal relationship is an 'intergenerational community of those who live out a radical vision of covenant', and that 'Deuteronomy always has its eyes on the children, on the coming generation.'[16] As such, Moses made it clear that children should be included in hearing the summons to love the Lord with every part of their life (Deut. 6.4–9) and gave advice as to how 'a child's imaginative horizon is completely pervaded by signs and reminders' of these commandments.[17] When this covenant is renewed at Moab, Moses gathers everyone together, including the children before the Lord (Deut. 29.10–11). He also commands the priests and the elders to gather everyone every seven years during the Festival of Booths to read out the law; it is specifically mentioned that this is partly for the benefit of the children who have not heard it before (Deut. 31.12–13; see also Ex. 12.26–27 and Josh. 8.34–35). Making sure that children know their own faith story *and* their part in it was an essential aspect of festivals and different gatherings, but also a normal expectation for adults in the community to pass this story to the next generation (e.g. Ps. 78.4, 145.4).

Children were also included in how the faith community continued to encounter God and in how they witnessed God at work. When King Jehoshaphat was informed that the Moabites, Ammonites and Meunites were coming to attack Judah, he stood in the 'assembly' and prayed to God, and we are told that 'all Judah stood before the LORD, with their little ones, their wives, and their children' (2 Chron. 20.13). Together they witnessed the Spirit coming upon one of their members who said, 'Thus says the LORD to you: "Do not fear or be dismayed at this great multitude; for the battle is not yours but God's. ... " Do not fear or be dismayed; tomorrow go out against them, and the LORD will be with you' (2 Chron. 20.15–17). Children themselves see God's Spirit at work. They see the present action of God in the world, they witness his promise and his help, and they see his guidance and his faithfulness. The story becomes their story in a very real way. It is no longer a story they hear and pass on – they now become the story as it shapes their life and as they realize how they in turn can shape the story of God and his people.

Similarly, a few years later, Joel calls on the priests to gather the people of God in a solemn assembly to fast and repent (Joel 2.15). This gathering is specifically to include children and those nursing at the breast (v. 16): 'no one is exempt from the call'.[18] Children are not bystanders, observing the response of adults to God and the response of God to adults – they are included in the response of the whole faith community, including repentance, and in the watching and waiting for God to come and save them. They are not left in a room together with their crayons while the adults do the serious business of repenting, lamenting and watching, for they too play a part in the covenant. Years later they are also included in the great rejoicing of Jerusalem in the dedication of the city wall (Neh. 12.43). Therefore, we see that children are not simply present at gatherings but take a full part in responding to God at these gatherings – their voices are heard in the repenting, lamenting and rejoicing. They become participants rather than spectators of the covenantal story of God and his people, and their contribution is not distinct from that of the adults in the community.

Children also feature in how God chooses to convey his message to Israel in Isaiah. Jacqueline Lapsley writes that 'images of safe, happy children are a principal means of expressing what God's salvation looks like – in stark contrast to the war Israel wages upon its own children.'[19] Furthermore, not only are children an important way to convey the divine message of salvation, they are also 'central to salvation', for 'how children are treated, both in the present and in the future, is essential to the divine vision of what God would have for Israel.'[20] Children are not overlooked by God. They have an important role in how God communicates with his people, and they are part of God's vision for salvation.

As we read through Scripture, we learn that God also calls different children to participate not simply by joining in with the rest of the people of God, but by taking a specific role in leading, teaching or revealing something of God to the rest of the faith community. For example, Samuel, who is dedicated by his mother Hannah to the house of the Lord after he is weaned, is called by God as a boy (1 Sam. 1.9–11, 19–28, 3.1–21). Interestingly, this happens before Samuel knew the Lord and the Word of the Lord (1 Sam. 3.7), but this does not make God hesitate in calling him and shows that Samuel's 'authorization' is 'rooted in nothing other than the freedom and promise of God'.[21] This perhaps challenges our expectations that children (and adults) need to reach a certain level of knowledge and depth of faith before they can be called by God. We also see that whereas Samuel is at first reliant on Eli for knowing how to respond to the Lord (v. 9), Eli then becomes dependent upon Samuel for knowing God's Word (vv. 15–18). For all of Eli's mistakes, he nevertheless has the wisdom and grace both to help a child discern God's call and then to humbly receive God's proclamation from this child. This passage shines a critical light onto our church today, asking if we are willing both to invest in our children to help them discern their call and God's Word, and to receive the ministry of our children. For Samuel, this is the start of a lifetime of ministry of hearing and proclaiming the Lord's Word, and of knowing that the Lord was with him (1 Sam. 3.19–21).

Samuel grows up to play an important role in the life and calling of another young boy, David, son of Jesse, who is the youngest of all his brothers. He is anointed by Samuel as a boy to be the next King of Israel, and 'the spirit of the LORD came mightily upon David from that day forward' (1 Sam. 16.13). He was an unlikely candidate, 'with no claim to make and no credentials to present'.[22] Thus, as his seven other brothers were presented before Samuel, he was left out in the fields (16.11). It becomes clear that the Lord has not chosen any of them, and so everyone waits for David to join their gathering, and when he does, the Lord declares, 'this is the one' (v. 12). An earlier verse tells us that the Lord was not looking at the outward appearance, but rather upon the heart (v. 7), and in the next chapter we see that David has interpreted his safety in protecting the sheep from wild animals as a sign of God's deliverance. He is already able to interpret and understand his life through the lens of faith where he knows that the Lord delivers (17.37). As such, David seems to know more of God than Samuel did as a young boy. Nevertheless, as Esther Menn writes: 'the child does not need to be instructed into a mature faith nor mentored until he qualifies to lead'.[23] In time David becomes the recognized King of Israel (2 Sam. 2.4), and we have many narratives of his leadership that demonstrate his mistakes as well as his zealous commitment to God.

One of the most well-known narratives of David occurs when he is still a young boy. As we read of him defeating the Philistine Goliath, the narrative mentions four times that he is a 'youth' (1 Sam. 17.33, 42, 55 and 58, using the Hebrew, *na'ar*). The NRSV translates this word in different ways, giving a progression from Saul exclaiming that he is 'just a boy' (v. 33), to Goliath's offence that his rival is 'only a youth' (v. 42), and finally to Saul's questioning the identity of this 'young man' (vv. 55, 58). These are valid translations of the Hebrew term *na'ar* but the way in which there is a progression from disbelief in 'just a boy' to wonder in the 'young man' suggests a valid interpretative move: that pre-victory David's youth is looked down upon, and post-victory it is championed. There is a shift in perspective about what a youth can achieve: as a young boy, nothing; as a young man, everything. David's age, however, has not changed in this narrative. He was a youth when he approached Goliath with sling in hand and a youth when he walked away with Goliath's head in his hand. It is worth asking ourselves and our churches how we view age, and how the language we use to describe people may reveal our attitude towards their usefulness and value, their potential and their gifts. Explicitly, we need to ask if we think our children are 'just' children.

This narrative also emphasizes David's faith. In his bold speech to Saul, justifying why he can go against Goliath (vv. 34–37), he first tells of his belief in his own skills (17.34–36), before proclaiming his belief that the Lord will save him 'from the hand of this Philistine' as he has done before 'from the paw of the lion and from the paw of the bear' (v. 37). Conversely, he declares that the Lord will deliver Goliath into his hand (vv. 46–47). David is confident that the Lord will deliver him from the hand of those who seek to harm him and will instead deliver them into his hand; but this is not to prove David's worth, but that 'all the earth may know that there is a God in Israel' (v. 46). David's concern is that Goliath is defying the God of the armies of Israel (vv. 26, 36, 45). Whereas the other Israelites claim that Goliath has come to 'defy Israel' (v. 25), David sees it as defying 'the armies of the living God' (v. 26) and therefore Chapman comments that he has a 'theocentric understanding of the threat Goliath poses'.[24] This contrast between David and the adults assembled is not insignificant. David's clarification that the threat is not against Israel but against the *God* of Israel involves just a few words and can easily be overlooked, but it signals a very different perspective and understanding of Israel's relationship with God, and vice versa. Brueggemann writes that the 'narrative has been arranged so that the weighty theological affirmation is placed in the mouth of David alone'.[25] We are challenged to consider if we listen carefully enough to our children to see how they might be bringing a theological perspective that we have not yet seen or understood. Children can be theologians as well as adults; we need to make sure we create the space to hear their voice, and in hearing, make sure we grasp their own theologizing of church and of the world.

Many other children in the Bible hold pivotal roles in the development of God's story with his people, some more obvious than others. For example, it was the concern and quick thinking of the girl Miriam that led to the return of her baby brother Moses to his mother for nursing (and which also resulted in her mother being paid for doing so) before he was then taken by the Pharaoh's daughter to be nurtured inside the palace (Ex. 2.1–10). The unnamed Israelite enslaved girl in 2 Kings 5 only features in a couple of verses, but it is through her actions that Naaman (the commander of the army of the King of Aram) declares that the God of Israel is the real God (5.15). Even though this young girl has been taken captive by Naaman's army and now finds herself as the servant of his wife, when she discovers Naaman is suffering from leprosy she tells her mistress about Elisha, who could heal him (5.3).

There are two signs of a remarkable, faithful character here. First, even though the Lord did not deliver her, she is confident that the Lord would be able to deliver Naaman from his illness via the prophet Elisha. Second, even though she has experienced terrible trauma at the hands of Naaman, she chose neither to delight in his suffering, nor to enjoy the power she could have grasped in not sharing information about his potential healing. Instead, she chooses to help her captors: 'If only my lord were with the prophet who is in Samaria! He would cure him of his leprosy' (v. 3). The words, 'if only' demonstrate her concern and her wish for Naaman's healing, but perhaps she

> also wants to make known the power for life that is among her own people ... In a time of killing and destruction, she focuses her attention on healing and restoration, even for the military leader on the other side.[26]

In exploring the stories of David as a boy and this enslaved girl, Menn highlights that

> both stories depict young people finding solutions to problems, intervening when adults are threatened and ineffectual, offering theological insights into God's ways, and acting within the context of international conflict and tensions between cultures and national identities.[27]

A shepherd boy and a servant girl: both acting with courage, concern and faith, and both promoting God's story of salvation and helping to replace fear with joy.

When we move into the New Testament, we see that children feature many times in Jesus' own ministry. Although they are often the recipients of his healing, they are important in revealing Jesus' divinity.[28] One child in particular stands out, for he does not require healing but provides Jesus with the means to perform another miracle in which thousands of people are fed (John 6.5–14). Jaison writes:

> From an unnoticed, unimportant presence, the boy in the multitude becomes a partner with Jesus by sharing his provisions to feed them (John 6.5–13) ... We envision the child standing in the midst to have dignity as God's agent and message, and not as a passive, helpless recipient of our sympathy.[29]

Many of us would love to know the conversation that happened between the boy and Andrew (who told Jesus about the boy). We do know that Andrew was quite flummoxed by the offering, asking, 'What are they among so many people?' (v. 9). I have often imagined the boy opening his lunch box and offering the first-century equivalent of a fish finger sandwich so that everyone could enjoy a feast. However, five loaves and two fish would be a large lunch for one young boy; perhaps he was carrying a picnic lunch for his whole family, or maybe he found himself caught up in the crowd while he carried this food home. Either way, if the miracle did not happen, if he handed over the food and never saw it again, then there is not only a risk of hunger to himself but also to his family (with the possibility of reproach). There is a slight echo here with the young boy in 1 Kings 17.8–16. In this passage, the young boy is also without a name or voice, and he and his widowed mother are hungry. God instructs Elijah to ask them for some food even though they only have enough oil and flour to make one final, small meal. Amazingly, they share the little they have, and God rewards their generosity and trust by multiplying their flour and oil so that they have an unending supply. Like the leftover fragments of bread that filled 12 baskets (John 6.13), the widow and the boy have leftover flour and oil with jars that are never empty (1 Kings 17.16).

In both passages the young boy plays a significant role in partnering with God so that others may see God's abundant provision. The young boy in John 6 was surely not the only person in the crowd who had food with them, and yet he was the one who came forward to give what he had to Jesus. His generosity might have been seen as foolish by some, but in the hands of Jesus his generosity unlocks a great miracle. It is a reminder never to see the offering of children as small or pointless, and to receive their offering with the expectation that God can do great things with it for the whole crowd.

## Summary

Children have always been important in the life of God's people. Throughout the Old Testament, the expectation was that they should receive the story of God's salvation and faithfulness from their elders, and that they, in turn, should pass it on to the next generation. Because they were included and actively engaged in the gatherings of God's people, especially at key points in their covenantal relationship with God, they witnessed God's powerful presence and his promises coming true. They heard about God *and* experienced God themselves. The story was not simply passed down through the words of their mouth but through the response of their heart, soul and might. As such, not only were the children shaped by the faith story they received, but the ongoing faith story itself was shaped by them. Furthermore, throughout Scripture children have partnered with God in specific ways, using their gifts or skills, or their faith and courage, to help others (either within the faith community or outside it) to hear and experience God themselves.

This section raises key questions about how we nurture children's faith in church today. For example, how do we encourage intergenerational gatherings that seek not only to remind every member of the faithfulness of God, but also to help each member encounter God's faithfulness today? Our children must be included in the ongoing discernment of God's will and ways in the world, and in the corporate response to God, whether that is one of repentance, lament or praise. How can we create a culture where the adults are ready to learn from children (like Eli and Samuel) and receive the theological perspectives that they can bring to how we navigate our way through contemporary challenges and situations (like Saul and David)? We need to ask how we value youth and see potential in our children, how we create space for them to exercise their faith, wisdom and courageous generosity (like that of the enslaved girl), and how we react to their offerings, even if our first reaction might be like that of Andrew's to the boy's lunch offering.

## Conclusion

This scriptural overview of the nature of church, the importance of fellowship, and of how children were called by God and put their faith into action, strongly points to the importance of intergenerational communities. A common thread running through this chapter has been the fact that children and adults together have worshipped, discerned, ministered, encountered God and responded to God, so that they, together, either as the people of the covenant or as the body of Christ, are shaped by God's salvation story. In fact, intergenerational relationships have not simply been a thread, but the spark for faith and vocation to grow. Growth in faith happens when all ages are together. But it is also true that growth in fellowship across the generations happens when faith is at the centre. In the next two chapters we will explore the hallmarks of intergenerational faith communities and how the contemporary church can be a place of nurture, fellowship and vocation for all ages together. As such, we will first look at how we can learn and inhabit the faith story together (Chapter 4), and second at how we can worship and use our gifts together for the spiritual formation of the whole church (Chapter 5).

## Notes

1 For example, the following reports: *Children in the Way* (General Synod Board of Education, 1988); *All God's Children?* (General Synod 988, 1991); *Youth a Part* (Church of England Board of Education, 1996); *Rooted in the Church* (Church of England Board of Education, 2016); *Faith in the Nexus* (NICER at Canterbury Christ Church University, 2020); and S. E. Holmes, 'The changing nature of ministry amongst children and families in the UK during the Covid-19 pandemic', *Christian Education Journal*, 19 1 (2022), pp. 134–51.

2 D. Clinton, N. Genders and D. Male, 2019, 'Growing faith: churches, schools and households', (GS 2121), General Synod of the Church of England, The Archbishops' Council, p. 1.

3 Clinton, Genders and Male, 'Growing faith', pp. 2, 5.

4 A. T. Lincoln, 1990, *Ephesians,* Word Biblical Commentary, vol. 42, Grand Rapids, MI: Zondervan, p. 162.

5 For a brief explanation of this statement, see A. E. McGrath, 1991, *I Believe: Exploring the Apostles' Creed*, Leicester: InterVarsity Press, pp. 110–13.

6 B. R. Gaventa, 2016, *When in Romans: An Invitation to Linger with the Gospel according to Paul*, Grand Rapids, MI: Baker Academic, p. 105.

7 D. Bonhoeffer, 1995, *The Cost of Discipleship*, trans. R. H. Fuller 1937, New York: Touchstone, p. 241.

8 See, for example, 1 Cor. 1.2, 15.9; 2 Cor. 1.1; Gal. 1.13; 1 Thess. 2.14; 2 Thess. 1.4; and Rom. 16.16.

9 M. Bockmuehl, 1997, *The Epistle to the Philippians*, London: A & C Black, p. 106.

10 N. Drake and B. Drake, 2021, *Worship for Everyone: Unlocking the Transforming Power of All-Age Worship*, London: SPCK, p. 42.

11 B. Witherington III, 1998, *The Acts of the Apostles: A Socio-Rhetorical Commentary*, Grand Rapids, MI: Eerdmans, p. 160.

12 As Witherington aptly writes, '*ekklēsia without koinōnia* in both spirit and substance is neither an adequate nor an accurate representation of what we are called to be' (p. 93, note 32). In B. Witherington III, 1995, *Conflict and Community in Corinth: A Socio-Rhetorical Commentary on 1 and 2 Corinthians*, Grand Rapids, MI: Eerdmans.

13 D. Bonhoeffer, 2015, *Life Together*, trans. J. W. Doberstein 1949, London: SCM Press, p. 8.

14 Bonhoeffer, *Life Together*, p. 26.

15 Lincoln, *Ephesians*, p. 162.

16 W. Brueggemann, 2001, *Deuteronomy*, Nashville, TN: Abingdon Press, pp. 84, 85.

17 Brueggemann, *Deuteronomy*, p. 85.
18 E. Achtemeier, 1996, *Minor Prophets I*, NIBC, Carlisle: Paternoster Press, p. 142.
19 J. E. Lapsley, 2008, '"Look! The children and I are as signs and portents in Israel": children in Isaiah', in M. J. Bunge (ed.), *The Child in the Bible*, Grand Rapids, MI: Eerdmans, pp. 82–102, p. 102.
20 Lapsley, 'Look! The children and I are as signs and portents in Israel', p. 102.
21 W. Brueggemann, 1990, *First and Second Samuel*, Louisville, KY: John Knox Press, p. 27.
22 Brueggemann, *First and Second Samuel*, p. 122.
23 E. M. Menn, 2008, 'Child characters in biblical narratives: the young David (1 Samuel 16–17) and the little Israelite servant girl (2 Kings 5:1–19)', in Bunge, *Child in the Bible*, pp. 324–52, p. 329.
24 S. B. Chapman, 2016, *1 Samuel as Christian Scripture: A Theological Commentary*, Grand Rapids, MI: Eerdmans, p. 154.
25 Brueggemann, *First and Second Samuel*, pp. 128–9.
26 Menn, 'Child characters in biblical narratives', p. 344.
27 Menn, 'Child characters in biblical narratives', p. 325.
28 For example, John 4.43–54; Luke 7.11–17, 24–30 (see also Matt. 15.21–28); Luke 8.40–42, 49–56 (also Matt. 9.18, 23–26; Mark 5.21–24, 35–43); Luke 9.37–43 (also Matt. 17.14–20; Mark 9.14–29).
29 J. Jaison, 2022, 'Affirming children's dignity as a theological vision and mandate', in R. Tan, N.A. Patellar and L.A. Hefford (eds), *God's Heart for Children: Practical Theology from Global Perspectives*, Carlisle: Langham Global Library, pp. 13–24, p. 22.

# 4

# Intergenerational Church: Learning and Growing Together

EMMA L. PARKER

The previous chapter revealed the importance of the intergenerational faith community in acting as a catalyst for children to live out the salvation story and to offer their faith and gifts to help the whole community. Throughout Scripture we see that it is through this intergenerational community that children not only hear about God's past acts of deliverance but also partake in discerning his ongoing work and responding to it accordingly. In the Old Testament and the New Testament, children are included in seeing how God guides his people through his Spirit and how he provides in different ways. They themselves witness God's work and so the story they pass to their children is not simply a story of their ancestors, but one of their own lives. These children were not herded into a separate side room and invited to colour a picture of God's faithfulness; they were asked to join the whole company of God's gathered people in meeting the Lord. Here they learned firsthand of God's faithfulness and they themselves became the picture of God's faithfulness. This experience enabled them to put their faith into action and thus find confidence in knowing how to interpret their own experience of life through the lens of faith (like David), how to offer their faith-shaped wisdom (like the servant girl) or their own gifts to God (like the boy with the lunch).[1] In this chapter, we will focus on the importance of today's church as an intergenerational community, before exploring how churches may engage with intergenerational learning so that all ages may grow together in faith.

## Intergenerational communities, identity and purpose

Roseline Olumbe argues that belonging to a community is 'critical' for children and points to the African principle of *ubuntu*, which is how an all-age community cares for each member and strives to 'enhance the happiness and quality of life' among all members.[2] Key aspects of *ubuntu* include an attitude of mutual support, the importance of relationships within the community, and reconciliation. It embodies a sense of collective responsibility to look after each other, including the children, and is instrumental in how children learn the values that are important to that community.[3]

In societies and cultures where a more individualistic approach drives how people view community and their role in it, the idea of a community's purpose being to build each other up (including children) is at risk of being lost. I have lived in some areas where neighbours in the same street do not know each other's names and travel out of their area to shop, socialize and worship. I visit families who live on large, new housing estates that have no community hall, recreation area or shops. Sometimes, these places can tap into an already present individualistic outlook and breed a sense of apathy towards belonging and contributing to a community. Sometimes, there can be fear about getting to know others and in being known. It might be important *not* to be known for those who feel vulnerable, who have not had a good experience of working with those in different professional authorities and who fear decisions being made about them. Trust is deeply important in committing to *ubuntu*, and when it is not there, isolation, individualism, fear of others and loneliness can take root.

However, I have also worked in areas where people have lived for generations in the same village or town, or where people take a communal pride in looking after each other. Once when

I was sitting in the living room of a family, leading some baptism preparation with two young siblings, I became aware of a steady stream of children coming and going. When I saw a boy carrying a plate of food with him as he left the house, the mum, seeing my puzzled expression, laughed and said that every afternoon she would cook a large pan of food, and the children in the street knew they could come in and help themselves. This single mum brought up her boys while working long shifts in the local care home, and yet she thought nothing of caring for the other children on her street. To her, they were all family.

For our churches to nurture the faith of our children, we need all-age faith communities that safely operate a vision of corporate care and responsibility in building up the whole community, and where safeguarding is seen as an essential and normal part of discipleship. In growing as an intergenerational church, where we learn, worship and minister together, we must pay attention to creating a healthy church culture where all members see safeguarding as their responsibility, where training is regularly undertaken and where policies are viewed not as restricting ministry but as enabling healthy growth in safe spaces. Creating these all-age communities, however, might culturally be very challenging in areas where having a sense of responsibility of care for each other is alien, or where trust and openness are costly and difficult. It might socially be very challenging in churches where the elderly fear children because of local news reports about teenagers and knife crime, or where the families have experienced criticism from older generations for how they are parenting. Stereotypes, generalizations and accusations can abound in churches when fear fuels how we relate across the generations, when we fail to take the time to know and love each other, and when we are anxious that the presence of another generation might mean we lose something we cherish.

If we are serious, however, about enabling faith to grow in all dimensions, then we need to be serious about enabling our churches to be intergenerational and creating a community where there is mutual care, learning and serving across the generations. In some societies, this will provide quite a countercultural community; in others, the church might need to learn from its neighbours. Becoming an intergenerational community of faith involves a journey of change, either because only one generation exists in the church, or because while multiple generations are present, they do not know how to talk to, worship alongside, serve and learn from each other. In these multigenerational spaces, there can be recognition of, and delight in, the presence of different ages, but genuine interaction is limited across them. The default for these churches is to provide age-based spaces for worship, fellowship and service, and then occasionally there are opportunities for these ages to come together (e.g. over coffee at the end of the service, or at the summer fair). The focus is largely on one generation: how to enable this generation to worship, how to recruit to positions of service from this generation, how to meet the spiritual, physical and relational needs of this generation.

In contrast, as it will become evident through this chapter and the next, intergenerational faith communities are those where the default is to grow in faith by all ages and generations meeting regularly together in the name of Christ. There is a recognition in these intergenerational communities that God works through all ages to bring about faith formation and growth, an eagerness to witness God speaking and ministering through different generations, and a humility to serve and receive the gifts and faith of those of different generations. Practically, these intergenerational faith communities provide space for genuine interaction between generations to foster care and enable mutual learning and serving within all aspects of church life. As Allen and Barnett write: 'The trajectory from multi- to inter- involves a greater depth of relationship, a change in the nature of the relationship, and an increasing openness to being changed through relationship with the "other".'[4] Hence, intergenerational churches regularly gather all ages together to worship, pray and encourage each other in discipleship, and they recognize, value and enable the gifts of each generation to be used in the edification of the whole body and for the mission of the church. Moreover, intergenerational churches expect deeper, transformational encounters with God when all ages engage in worship and discipleship together. Age-based groups might still meet for specific reasons, but the focus is on bringing the generations together to be a transformed and transforming community.

Westerhoff argues that 'true community necessitates the presence and interaction of three generations'.[5] He then explains that the third generation (those of an older age) is the 'generation of memory', the second is the 'generation of the present' and the first is 'potentially the generation of vision'. However, he also believes that each generation needs the other in order to offer this gift, whereby vision needs memory, and that only having a generation of the present leads to a life that 'becomes intolerable and meaningless'.[6] Each generation needs the other to provide a meaningful and growing community and, I would add, to provide identity, and purpose. This somewhat echoes the prophecy in Joel, which Peter declares is fulfilled as the Holy Spirit was poured out upon the Disciples at Pentecost: 'your sons and your daughters shall prophesy, your old men shall dream dreams, and your young men shall see visions' (Joel 2.28; see Acts 2.14–21). We are presented with a picture of different generations filled with the Spirit and working together to uncover and interpret the reality of the present day, seeing how God may transform it and imagining the journey from perceiving potential to tasting glory.

This seems to be what Brueggemann writes of when he argues that worship should be an 'act of poetic imagination', for the poetic imagination paints the 'alternative world' that counters the current contemporary one of injustice.[7] He writes: 'The practice of such poetic imagination that invites us playfully to alternative reality is deeply rooted in old texts, old memories, and old practices; it nonetheless requires contemporary, disciplined, informed imagination to sustain alternative vision.'[8] For Brueggemann, this interplay of imagination, understanding the present reality and holding on to the corporate memory that tells of God's justice and faithfulness (through the 'old texts, old memories, and old practices') enables a faith community to maintain its distinctive and countercultural identity of being a holy community. Thus, whether we use Westerhoff's language of vision-present-memory brought about by the interaction of three generations, or Brueggemann's (alternative) vision-reality-memory brought about by poetic imagination, we see that one of the purposes (or at least consequences) of the faith community gathering is to hold together, through the Spirit, the past, present and future story of God with his people. There is a Spirit-filled simultaneous looking back and looking forward, while being fully aware of God's work in the present. It needs the Spirit, and the interaction of different generations, to enable a faith community to uncover reality and to prophesy, to see visions and dream dreams.

The significance of this for our current exploration is that this function of the faith community builds its (countercultural) identity and purpose, and in so doing, gives its different members a sense of belonging to each other and of needing each other. In their research with teenagers and emerging adults, Kara Powell, Jake Mulder and Brad Griffin propose that the key questions teenagers are asking are, 'Who am I?', 'Where do I fit?' and 'What difference do I make?'[9] In other words, they are asking questions of identity, belonging and purpose. Thus, if we heed the need for the church to bring together past, present and future, inspired by the Spirit and enabled by the different generations, then this also creates the space for children and teenagers to ask and find answers to these questions of identity, belonging and purpose.

This is exactly what I found when I was a teenager in church. When I was 15, I started going to a course at my local parish church aimed at helping people explore the Christian faith. I was the only teenager among mostly older people who were already part of the congregation, but I was entranced both by hearing their real stories of faith, and by the way they welcomed, accepted, loved and cared for me. It was the first time I had heard anyone talk about how Jesus would help them in the present, and so their stories helped me to connect my threadbare knowledge of the faith story (mainly of the Gospels) with present-day discipleship. I felt as though the pages of the Bible came alive in these older people's lives, and I remember thinking, 'I want what you've got.' Thus began my journey to deepen my understanding and experience of faith, of joining the stories of years ago to our story today and of finding my own identity within this wonderful, local and cosmic story that included looking back and forward, connecting the generations of memory, present and vision.

The actions of this community were not that radical, but their ethos and attitude towards me felt radical. I was invited to something that was free, accepted for who I was and not what I could achieve, listened to with patience and interest, and treated like everyone's granddaughter. When one person made me a birthday cake for my 16th birthday and they all sang for me, it was an unexpected delight to receive such care and attention, and I remember the joy and relief in realizing that I belonged to this community. For me, this community provided a safer, more loving and accepting space than any other I had belonged to, and it was here that I found identity and purpose.

## Belonging and belief

This experience also made me feel as if I had become part of another family, and therefore gave me a wonderful sense of belonging. This is what Powell, Mulder and Griffin argue is important in churches helping young people to choose and stay at their church, for churches must create 'an experience that feels like family'; in other words, an experience where belonging can be found.[10] The type of relationships on offer in building this 'family' experience is key, and should be characterized by a genuine interest in getting to know each other and a willingness to respond and care appropriately for each other once we have a greater appreciation of the challenges and joys each other carries. In their research, Powell, Mulder and Griffin found that children who were rooted in their church often used the following words to describe it: 'welcoming, accepting, belonging, authentic, hospitable, and caring'.[11] They called this the 'warmth cluster', which is more about the culture of the church than anything else: 'Warmth often lives much deeper than your programs and structures – it's the lifeblood coursing through the veins of your church body.'[12]

The importance of enabling these deeper intergenerational relationships is that they are crucial in helping children and teenagers to go deeper into their exploration of faith. Growing these relationships links with the growth of belief. Santos argues that when children are 'raised in a truly intergenerational environment defined by a pattern of intentional Christian practices', they gain a deeper sense of belief and belonging, which enables them to participate in a journey of faith in which all generations travel together.[13] Different research projects have shown the close relationship between belonging and belief. For example, Powell, Mulder and Griffin conclude that relationship leads to formation and belief: 'First relationship, then formation. First belonging, then belief.'[14] Voas and Crockett argue that a 'failure' in belonging 'has resulted in whole generations being less active and less believing than the ones that came before'.[15] For growth, therefore, we must focus both on belonging and believing.

From my own experience, I have found that if we use 'belonging then belief' to inform our mission strategy, we need to be intentional about helping people to make the journey to belief. Our churches may have a wonderful sense of belonging, but on closer inspection they may be operating more as a social club than a transformed and transforming faith community. Conversely, I have seen new people wander into church because they have had an encounter with God, have come to believe in him and have felt God nudging them to come to church. Their belief has led them to find belonging. Often it has been children who have compelled their parents to bring them to church because of their questions about faith. We therefore need to create churches where the journey can be made from belonging to belief, or belief to belonging, while also working to deepen the experience of, and participation in, both. Once again, it is imperative that in doing so we have good habits and policies of safeguarding and seek to create a healthy church culture in larger and smaller all-age gatherings.

# Learning and Growing Together

## 1 – *Experience and action*

For Westerhoff, the way to deepen belief and belonging lies in the church making sure that it acknowledges its ministry of education. He writes: 'The struggle to know, understand, interpret, live, and do God's Word must be at the centre of our educational mission', because 'unless the story is known, understood, owned, and lived, we and our children will not have Christian faith.'[16] In figuring out what this looks like in practical terms, he argues that 'the most significant and fundamental form of learning is experience'.[17] He gives as an example the fact that if we see our church seeking the good of others, then we will learn the story of the Good Samaritan (Luke 10.25–37). Thus, if our church always seeks to live out the teachings and way of the Bible, then our children will first learn God's Word through seeing it in action in the community. The second step is for children to be given the chance to act out their faith, to join with God in his works of social action, works of peace, justice and love.[18] In the context of belonging-believing, we might say that believing is deepened when those who belong to the faith community see the Bible story in action, are themselves shaped by the Bible story, and learn how to live out the Bible story through partnering with God.

Learning through experience and action is undoubtedly important, but without intentionally and obviously connecting it to our faith story, the learning could simply be that church is about being nice to others. We need this explicit connection because 'our theological learning requires the ability not only to make sense of the challenges and questions about the reality of faith, but also the ability and capacity to see things differently as a result of holding to faith.'[19] Additionally, we must ensure that within experience and action, we expect young and old to learn from each other. Any intergenerational learning opportunities need to be ones where children and young people are not only formed and nurtured in their faith, but also enabled to help shape the formation and discernment of the whole community themselves.[20]

However, intergenerational learning requires our churches to recognize that people of all ages learn in different ways: in practical, 'hands-on' experiences, in reflective activities or analytical opportunities, or in creative art. While some need facts, others need imagination; some need tangible objects, others need space for thinking; some need conversation, others need silence. Most people need a mixture of all of these, and the challenge is in creating a church community where all ages can learn together in a variety of ways, where the whole person is fed and enabled to love God and one's neighbour. Our churches have often offered this by creating different groups that would naturally appeal to different learners (e.g. a Bible study group, a craft group, a social action group). While each of these groups provides for a different learning preference, they do not necessarily cater for a variety of learning styles within them. Thus, another option would be to explore how each group that aims for intergenerational learning can do so in a way that includes a variety of learning styles within each group. For example, a social action group meeting to litter pick might begin their activity with a short act of worship, using Scripture that resonates with the activity (e.g. 1 Thess. 5.15–18; Phil. 4.8), singing a hymn that praises God as creator, and praying St Francis's prayer for God to make us instruments of his peace in creation.

## 2 – *Prayerfully reading and exploring the Bible*

Learning together across the generations may happen at different points during the week; it should be a thread that runs through many of our points, places and purposes of gathering, whether this is a litter pick or a midweek service. However, Bible study groups have traditionally been the way in which members can focus primarily on learning more about faith and discipleship by reading and exploring the Bible together. As such, our churches need to reflect on how these can be intergenerational learning spaces that seek to equip each member for discipleship in their daily life. For example, a Bible study group that includes a student who is taking part in their college production of *Joseph and the Amazing Technicolor Dreamcoat* might decide to study parts of the Joseph narrative in Genesis 37–50. Another group that includes a teenager who is the only Christian in her form class and is struggling to answer her friend's questions about Jesus, might decide to look at the 'I Am' sayings in John's Gospel, which might similarly help her mother (also in the group) who has just started to re-engage with her faith after a difficult period of grief.

These intergenerational groups must seek to include a range of styles for learning, reflecting and responding, and enable space for questions, exploration and sharing together. It is important for group members to know that doubt, wrestling and questions are not signs of a lack of faith, a failing faith or a disrespectful faith, but of a curious (and healthy) faith. It was curiosity that made Moses stop what he was doing to take a closer look at the burning bush, and when the Lord saw his curiosity he spoke to him and called him (Ex. 3.3–4). Children and young people (and adults) need to have the freedom to be curious, and have the safety to question, probe and examine without the rest of the group panicking or going into defence mode.

However, in exploring it is also important not to mine each passage for a 'moral punch line' for this can result in a 'behaviour-based gospel that feels a lot more like a list of dos and don'ts we must follow to please God than an invitation to participate in a beautiful story of God's transformative grace'.[21] The way in which curiosity and exploration are allowed to happen can be through a variety of modes, from using the arts (music, images, objects, clay) to quiet reflection, from talking in pairs to writing down thoughts on Post-it notes. Those who process information in different ways need a balance of times when the group is asked to ponder quietly and when to share aloud with a partner. As a matter of course, members might be given paper and pens so that those who learn and explore by writing and drawing can do so throughout the meeting and are given space to share their reflections in this way so that they know their contributions are also valuable.

Many Bible study groups use a method of reading the Bible together and then going through a series of set questions which aim to get underneath the surface of the text and to help members see how this living Word speaks afresh into their own lives. If the group is using a resource with set questions, then these questions will need to be edited to reflect the ages and life situations of the group; perhaps these questions can be prepared by two or three people who have experience of living or working with children and with older people. But, as long as the group is also attentive to different learning styles, then there is no reason why this traditional method of learning in a Bible study group could not be used for intergenerational groups.

Another possible method for an intergenerational Bible study group could be Anna Carter Florence's idea of 'rehearsing Scripture', where members meet to read, rehearse, and then say something true about this living Word.[22] Florence proposes that after reading the Bible passage together, members should then focus on the verbs rather than the nouns, for nouns often remind us 'that we're reading about a galaxy far, far away' which 'lets us keep our distance'.[23] Nouns can illustrate the differences between 'them' and 'us', whereas verbs cross boundaries of time and culture as 'you and I share verbs with Adam and Eve and Abraham and Sarah and Moses and Miriam and Ruth and Naomi'.[24] Verbs help us to step into Scripture and come back out again, seeing the relevance for discipleship today. Florence provides a guide as to what the group then does with the verbs, what questions to ask to explore not only the passage but how this connects to each member, and how we might hear God.[25]

The group then moves into 'rehearsing' the passage by stepping into and imagining the roles of the characters, or even by acting out the scene so that they can see details and perspectives that had not previously been seen.[26] Florence suggests members could try to change roles and make sure they step into the shoes of the different characters in the scene and allow time to ask new questions and try new things. And finally, having explored and lived in the text, the group moves to figure out how the reading and the seeing may lead to 'saying something true' so that the community of readers can become a 'community of speakers'.[27]

This type of Bible study might not be suitable for everyone, but it gives a creative and thorough way of learning together, drawing from different styles of learning and offering a very interactive way for members to learn from Scripture and from each other. It also gives the group a sense of purpose that extends beyond themselves. This way of reading Scripture is accessible to all ages and all stages of faith and experience; the person new to faith and the person who has previously attended decades of Bible study groups can participate equally together. It would enable all ages to learn the faith story and inhabit it, while being open to seeing how God might move the group to prophetically speak the living Word into the reality of the contemporary world.

A very different practice of prayerfully reading the Bible is *lectio divina*. This might suit an intergenerational group as it helps members to imaginatively and prayerfully enter the passage not as a method for studying the Bible, but as a way to deeply listen to God, contemplate what they have heard together and reflect on how this shapes their daily lives at school, at work and at home.[28] In this way of prayerfully reading Scripture, the passage is read aloud slowly, and then the words or phrases that capture the attention of the mind or heart are mulled over, explored and shared in the group. It is a practice that 'needs to be imbued with an understanding and expectation that God is active and present', not just as the group meet together, but as each member carries this moment into the rest of their lives, for it is a 'lifestyle rather than a method'.[29] A doctoral student exploring intergenerational spiritual formation found that when *lectio divina* was used by an intergenerational group, the children described how they felt they were growing in confidence in understanding how the Bible resonates with them. Additionally, the adults realized their involvement was not about helping children in their faith, but about being fellow partners in 'learning and growing' together.[30]

As the different generations meet to learn in different contexts and for different purposes, we must attend not only to different learning styles and life events that each age might be facing but also to the importance of reciprocity. In such learning environments, we need to have the humility and the joyful expectation that children, young people and adults are learners and teachers together, sitting at the feet of Jesus together, prayerfully learning the habits of Jesus together, and putting knowledge into action as we grow in faith together.

## Conclusion

It is easy to assume that our investment in creating intergenerational communities is for the benefit of children and teenagers, so that they have the best chance of finding opportunities to learn more about their faith, to understand how it shapes their life and how it can provide meaning, and for them to explore the important questions of identity, belonging and purpose. However, current research shows that 'intergenerational experiences contribute uniquely to sustainable, long-term faith formation across all ages'.[31] In other words, young and old and everyone in between benefit from living faith together as a body made up of different generations who share together in the faith story, who are shaped together by the faith story and who are transformed together by the faith story. Indeed, Lucy Moore argues that these all-age church communities are 'the best way of growing disciples'.[32]

I know that my own faith grows because of my older and younger siblings in Christ. When I sit with a 95-year-old who tells me how much they love Jesus and how God has always helped them through life, my faith grows by hearing their testimony. When a four-year-old tells me that when we prayed they heard God say to them, 'You are made of nothing but love', my faith in God is strengthened, and I marvel and wonder at the tender delight God has for this child. I wholeheartedly agree, therefore, that faith 'is not just passed *down*. It's passed *around*.'[33] If we believe in the church as the body of Christ, made up of many different members, all needing each other to grow in love and in faith, then we need to believe that the body functions and grows when all ages learn how to live together as the body of Christ. If our different members always learn in age-based groups, then there is never going to be any meaningful or fruitful cross-generational reciprocity in supporting and helping each other. Thus, while the different members of the body may appear to be joined, they may in fact only be held together superficially by sticky tape.

In the previous chapter, we saw that integral to the church community is the concept of *koinōnia*, which describes the type of sharing relationship between members. This *koinōnia* or fellowship goes beyond acquaintanceship to a kinship. Where I grew up in the north-east of England, the term 'marra' is used to describe someone who is very close to you. It comes from the local pronunciation for 'marrow' and expresses the idea that the companionship of this person 'has a meaning so deep and essential that it's felt in the bones'.[34] As we build our intergenerational churches, where two or three (or more) generations join together as the body of Christ, we must strive for these generations to know each other closely and have a companionship so essential that they may learn how to live as people of faith, move together as one, and be transformed together by the Spirit. We need intergenerational churches that are marra communities: growing in faith and growing closer together.

## Notes

1 See the previous chapter for an exploration of these narratives in 1 Samuel 17; 2 Kings 5 and John 6.

2 R. Olumbe, 2022, '*Ubuntu*: conceptualizing community for children in the African context', in R. Tan, N. A. Patellar and L. A. Hefford (eds), *God's Heart for Children: Practical Theology from Global Perspectives*, Carlisle: Langham Global Library, pp. 75–86, p. 76.

3 Many other cultures embody this understanding of community. For example, we see this in the passage where Mary and Joseph mistakenly believe that the young Jesus is with others from their wider community (Luke 2.41–51).

4 H. C. Allen and C. Barnett, 2018, 'Addressing the two intergenerational questions', in H. C. Allen (ed.), *InterGenerate: Transforming Churches through Intergenerational Ministry*, Abilene, TX: Abilene Christian University Press, pp. 17–23, p. 18.

5 J. H. Westerhoff, 2012, *Will Our Children Have Faith?*, third edition, New York: Morehouse Publishing, p. 53.

6 Westerhoff, *Will Our Children Have Faith?*, p. 53.

7 W. Brueggemann, 2007, *Mandate to Difference: An Invitation to the Contemporary Church*, Louisville/London: Westminster John Knox Press, p. 117.

8 Brueggemann, *Mandate to Difference*, p. 117.

9 K. Powell, J. Mulder and B. Griffin, 2016, *Growing Young: Six Essential Strategies to Help Young People Discover and Love Your Church*, Grand Rapids, MI: Baker Books, p. 95.

10 Powell, Mulder and Griffin, *Growing Young*, pp. 170–1.

11 Powell, Mulder and Griffin, *Growing Young*, p. 166. Nick and Becky Drake also propose that children need belonging, familiarity, acceptance, purpose and fun. In: N. Drake and B. Drake, 2021, *Worship for Everyone: Unlocking the Transforming Power of All-Age Worship*, London: SPCK, chap. 6.

12 Powell, Mulder and Griffin, *Growing Young*, p. 166.

13 J. B. Santos, 'Why now?', in Allen, *InterGenerate*, pp. 39–49, pp. 46–7. Conversely, he finds that when 'spiritual formation primarily takes place alongside one's own peers, a broader understanding of the church is distorted' (p. 46).

14 Powell, Mulder and Griffin, *Growing Young*, p. 171.

15 D. Voas and A. Crockett, 'Religion in Britain: neither believing nor belonging', *Sociology*, 39 1 (2005), pp. 11–28, p. 20.

16 Westerhoff, *Will Our Children Have Faith?*, p. 32.

17 Westerhoff, *Will Our Children Have Faith?*, pp. 61–2.

18 Westerhoff, *Will Our Children Have Faith?*, p. 62.

19 N. Shepherd, 2016, *Faith Generation: Retaining Young People and Growing the Church*, London: SPCK, p. 85.

20 See Shepherd, *Faith Generation*, p. 29.

21 Powell, Mulder and Griffin, *Growing Young*, p. 147.

22 A. C. Florence, 2018, *Rehearsing Scripture: Discovering God's Word in Community*, Norwich: Canterbury Press.

23 Florence, *Rehearsing Scripture*, p. 17.

24 Florence, *Rehearsing Scripture*, p. 19.

25 Depending on the group, the leader(s) might decide to prepare a list of all or some of the verbs in the passage and give this as a handout to the group to enable discussion.

26 Florence, *Rehearsing Scripture*, chap. 4.

27 Florence, *Rehearsing Scripture*, pp. 84, 85. Florence offers these six questions for this final section: 'What's the place in the text that gets you?', 'Why does it get you?', 'What do you know about God from this moment in the text that gets you?', 'Why does your community need to hear this today?', 'What do you want to say?' and 'What do you hope these words will do?' (chap. 6, 'Saying Something True').

28 This is an ancient practice that was often used in monastic prayer and developed in the twelfth century. See: E. de Waal, 2003, *Lost in Wonder: Rediscovering the Spiritual Art of Attentiveness*, Norwich: Canterbury Press, pp. 11–12.

29 G. New, 2015, *Imaginative Preaching: Praying the Scriptures so God Can Speak Through You*, Carlisle: Langham Global Library, p. 31.

30 H. C. Allen, C. Lawton, C. and C. L. Seibel, 2023, *Intergenerational Christian Formation: Bringing the Whole Church Together in Ministry, Community, and Worship*, Downers Grove, IL: InterVarsity Press, p. 196. Another option might be to use 'Dwelling in the Word', where members read a passage slowly while considering a couple of questions, then share their response first with a partner and then the whole group, and finally, the group discerns what God might be doing among them. For an example of how this method has helped intergenerational learning, see W. McCoy, 'All ages learning together', in Allen, *InterGenerate*, pp. 151–9.

31 Allen and Barnett, 'Addressing the two intergenerational questions', p. 17.

32 L. Moore, 2016, *All-Age Worship*, second edition, Abingdon: BRF, p. 35.

33 Powell, Mulder and Griffin, *Growing Young*, p. 174.

34 D. Jackson, 2019, *The Northumbrians: North-East England and Its People, A New History*, London: Hurst & Company, p. 8.

# 5

# Intergenerational Worship, Ministry and Vocation: Being Transformed Together

EMMA L. PARKER

In Chapter 3 we explored various scriptural passages that reveal the importance of children being present with adults in worshipping God, in praying, lamenting and rejoicing, in discerning God's voice and actions, in witnessing God working through others and being ready to respond with faith and trust. We also saw that intergenerational relationships were key in enabling children to offer their gifts, wisdom, insight and skills. For the child Samuel the older priest Eli was important (1 Sam. 3.8–9), for the child David it was Samuel (now as an older prophet) and King Saul (1 Sam. 16.1–13, 17.37), and for the boy with the fish and bread it was Andrew (one of the Disciples) and Jesus (John 6.1–13). Interestingly, for both Miriam and the servant girl, the adults who listened and acted on their advice were outside God's covenant people (Ex. 2.1–10; 2 Kings 5.1–5a). Intergenerational mutuality and reciprocity are key to the health and growth of the whole faith community.

This links with another previous insight in Chapter 3: the importance of *koinōnia* in the church community, whereby members experience partnership with God and with each other. For Christians, *koinōnia* (fellowship) is about tenderly and persistently caring for each member, making sure they are not alienated due to a lack of regard for their practical or spiritual needs, and seeking to love and build them up in their faith. However, we also found that it is about releasing others in ministry by recognizing that God calls each member to use their gifts, and that the whole body needs each member for the wider mission of God (e.g. Gal. 2.9). It is about a commitment to regularly meet together to worship and pray, in a way that builds up the whole body of Christ (Acts 2.42). Intergenerational faith communities must also seek for *koinōnia* to be a hallmark of how the whole body of Christ empowers and encourages each other across the generations to embrace their different vocations, engage in ministry together and to pray and worship together. Such intergenerational *koinōnia* has the power to 'contribute uniquely to sustainable, long-term faith formation across all ages'.[1]

This chapter will first focus on the importance of intergenerational worship, and it will offer some essential theological and practical ingredients in thinking about how to prepare, deliver and experience intergenerational worship. Gathering as the body of Christ to worship is central to the purpose of the whole body because it is from this that all other ministry and discipleship flow. This chapter will then focus on the importance of intergenerational ministry: how children can be edified in exploring their purpose and enabled to discern and use their gifts to share in the wider mission and ministry of the church.

## Worshipping together

Central to the life of the church is the act and art of worshipping as the one body of Christ. When churches can do this with all ages worshipping together in the same space, at the same time, then this body becomes a powerful witness to the reconciling power of God, who brings together our differences and, without erasing them, connects them together for goodness and beauty in this divided world. This powerful gathering should, therefore, be intentionally intergenerational: it should seek for all ages present to encounter God in their midst, be transformed by that encounter and sent out as a light to be a blessing in a world where

## INTERGENERATIONAL WORSHIP, MINISTRY AND VOCATION

darkness feeds off division and fear of difference. Miroslav Volf writes: 'It may not be too much to claim that the future of our world will depend on how we deal with identity and difference.'[2] He is primarily talking about cultural difference, but it can be applied to any difference, including age. If the worshipping community can be one where people of different ages are seen, valued and included in the one body of Christ, then this provides not only the world with a powerful view of how to 'deal with identity and difference', but also our children, teenagers and young people, who are and will be the peacemakers for several generations in our world. Intergenerational worship is therefore a 'spiritual force for good' not only in the faith community, but also in our wider communities across the world.[3]

Intergenerational worship must therefore truly be for all ages. It is neither a children's service where the adults can switch off, nor is it a service for adults with a few things thrown in 'for the children': a colouring sheet, a random puppet and a token child trying to read a Bible passage from Revelation. Nick and Becky Drake write that we need to elevate children and engage adults. In other words, we must place 'a high value on children ... worship *with* them and not *to* them' and we need to make sure we do not forget and overlook the adults in the room.[4] We need to visibly model our doctrines; if we believe that children are part of the body of Christ then we need to see that in action.

One way to do this is to ensure that, as with learning together (Chapter 4), intergenerational worship shows awareness not only of different ages and abilities, but also of the different styles of engaging with worship and learning. Those of us who plan and lead these services need to imagine our congregation and step into each aspect of our prepared service from their point of view. While we need to be wary of using too many stereotypes or generalizations, there are some age-based assumptions we can make that are fair to our worshipping members about how they may or may not be able to engage with our prepared service. For example, having too much written liturgy to follow, say or sing will mean that young (and some older) children will struggle to participate. If we have teachers in the congregation or good relationships with a local school, we could seek their advice about appropriate reading for different ages as well as checking with the parents and children in our church.

Furthermore, regardless of age, we will always have some members who are kinaesthetic learners, who need physical movement, touch and interaction to engage and participate in the different elements of worship. Our worship might therefore involve actions or sign language as we sing or pray, or we might invite people to write prayers on paper which they then attach to a prayer tree or peg on to a washing line around the pillars or communion rail. Some worshippers could be invited to the front to take part in a dramatic telling of the Bible passage, or to participate in an activity to help the preacher demonstrate a point in their sermon.

Rituals can also help as they enable our worship to be multi-sensory. As Smit writes, in intergenerational worship we need 'to be able to touch, see, smell, hear, and taste that the Lord is good'.[5] Rituals can help children and young people (and indeed, all ages) sense the mystery, the wonder and the otherness of God. They can help worshippers to enter this sacred space of worship, where we can metaphorically take off our shoes around the burning bush and realize we are standing on holy ground, for God is with us. It might be something as simple as a child 'lighting' an LED candle while the rest of the congregation says a refrain such as: 'We light this candle because Jesus is the light of the world.' Rituals, patterns and repetition are all good if they signal the sacred, point us to God's glory, and draw us into the faith story once again. Rituals in worship 'bring our sacred tradition and our lives together; providing us with both meaning and motivation for daily existence'.[6]

In putting together intergenerational worship, sometimes we simply need to reflect on the different balances in a service: is there a balance between movement and stillness, listening and interacting, predictability and spontaneity? Is there a balance between sound and silence, thinking on your own and sharing with others, and praise and lament? And, importantly, is there a balance between adults and children leading worship? Intergenerational worship is not only about making sure children are able to worship among adults, but also about offering them opportunities to lead with adults. We need to make sure that, where possible, all ages can help to prepare, lead and facilitate worship, where young and old can take part in the drama or sketch, and where different ages lead, read, preach and intercede. Depending on your congregation, this might not always be easy. You might only have a handful of pre-schoolers, or your teenagers might prefer to snorkel with jellyfish rather than stand in front of others with the attention upon them as they read or pray. In churches where there are few (or no) children and teenagers, it is important not to lose hope and to cling on to the vision of intergenerational worship, and to keep praying for growth. In other churches, the tendency can be for worship leaders to create (or be given) an expectation of perfection and the reins can be held quite tightly by a few people. In these situations, attitudes of humility, generosity and trust need to be grown, before meaningful change can happen.

When thinking of balance, we also need to consider how we might transition from one balance to another. For example, if we have an all-age Remembrance Sunday service which includes the two-minute silence, we need to think about how to introduce this to the congregation so that the children understand why this is important, and the parents know what to do if their two-year-old starts singing 'Baby Shark'! Signalling transitions (especially when there is a large contrast) not only helps children and parents, but also church members who are neurodivergent and others who would benefit from being eased into changes in pace, noise or levels of participation, rather than experiencing a rollercoaster of change within a short timeframe.

Intergenerational worship should therefore seek to 'intentionally include and draw in people of all ages – communicating through words and actions that each member of the body is important and is a blessing to the worshipping community'.[7] This act of inclusion will require the art of generosity. The motivation for worshipping in this kind of way needs to come primarily from a selfless place. I am not 'number one' in this service – the other person is, and I would narrow this further to say that our children and young people are. We have become accustomed to the option of choosing worship where I and my needs are at the centre, or where I can shape worship to my own preferences.[8] Intergenerational worship however, although it will benefit me and help to grow my faith, is not about me. It is about us, young and old, and as we have consistently seen in previous chapters, God works graciously through our children and young people to bless the whole community of faith. Furthermore, it is shaped around God's preferences, where the little children are welcomed and where everything else stops so they can be blessed.

As such, if intergenerational worship aligns with God's preference for inclusive worship that welcomes everyone, especially children and young people, then those who design and lead it should ensure that the worship space fosters a sense of God's presence. There needs to be an expectation from all worshippers that as we gather before God we will encounter God together. Our intergenerational worship needs to be 'deliberate in creating the spaces and practices that enable young people to experience God's presence'.[9] Whereas for Shepherd children need to 'learn' how to experience God, Smit argues that children are 'innately spiritual beings and experience the transcendent in their lives from their earliest days apart from any formal religious instruction'.[10] Indeed, children can often naturally sense the sacred in everyday life experiences, and Nye argues that 'spiritual awareness is especially natural and common in childhood'.[11]

Children, however, are all different with some being more aware of God's presence than others, and of course, they will feel and sense it in different ways. A few years ago, after leading a Christmas service in church for a local infant school (in which I had volunteered the teachers to act out the nativity story, to the delight of the children), I asked the children at the end what they enjoyed in the service. I received various responses, usually to do with when something funny had happened (often inadvertently), seeing their class teacher wearing a tea towel on their head with a toy sheep under their arm, or singing the carols. However, a little girl on her way out came over to me, tugged my arm and said, 'I liked being with God.' She took me by surprise, in a wonderful way. Embarrassingly, because most of these children did not attend church or come from 'church' backgrounds, I had not expected this response. I realized my expectations and assumptions in leading worship with children needed to change. My goal had been to try to teach the children about the birth of Jesus and help them to know how much God loves them. But I needed to widen the goal to hope for these children to be moved spiritually, to sense God and know God not only in their thoughts and knowledge, but also with their whole being. I've also had experiences where I have gently asked children if they heard anything from God or felt God's presence, only to receive blank faces and shrugs. It's therefore important not to make children feel like they have failed if they have not sensed God, but also to create spaces where they might.

This also means that it is important in our worship to be able to witness others experiencing God's presence and being 'real' before God. When my daughter was a toddler there was an occasion where she witnessed someone in church bringing faith and life together before God in quite a profound way. I had packed enough colouring books and raisins to see us through a whole week, and as the service rolled on, she was happily in her own world, seemingly disconnected from everyone else and the service. Until, that is, a church member in her 70s started leading the intercessions, and as she prayed for a tragedy that had just hit an overseas country, she started to weep. Her raw, spontaneous lament soaked her prayers. At this, my daughter looked up: she dropped her pencil and was mesmerized by the prayers. In an instant, she connected with worship at a level I had never seen before, as she and the intercessor encountered God together in lament. I realized that this was the first time my daughter had seen someone cry in church.

In our encounters with God during our worship together, we must be authentic and not afraid to express the full spectrum of our emotions and responses as we present ourselves and the needs of the world before our God. Although this was a spontaneous response of lament, our intergenerational worship could also include prepared moments where we hear the testimony of another worshipper in how they have encountered God in other ways during the week. Testimonies and real emotion, in response to encountering God in different spaces and situations, help to build the faith of the whole church, but also give permission to our children to do the same.

Thus far, in exploring how to enable worship that includes all ages, we have thought about different learning and worshipping styles, the need for balance and a spirit of generosity, and the importance of enabling God's presence to be known, felt and seen in each other. One final comment around intergenerational worship is that these services need to be overseen or coordinated by spirit-filled leaders who are sensitive to the movement of God among young and old, who are consciously praying for heaven to be on earth in this space, and who are persistently enabling all ages to sense and respond to the Spirit of God. There needs to be an expectation that not only will people encounter God, but that they will also be *transformed* by this encounter as we worship God together. This aim transcends all differences, uniting the congregation in a common purpose of experiencing and encountering God. Exploring what all-age worship looks like therefore makes us discover what it means 'to be an "all-people" church' and how to worship as such – indeed, it pushes us to 'ponder what God might want us to become'.[12] It is in intergenerational worship that we enable God to transform the whole body together, as we grow together in faith.

## Fellowship in the body: ministry and vocation

Chapter 3 noted the importance of children's skills, gifts and faith being used throughout Scripture to edify the people of God or point 'outsiders' to God's glory and power, and the importance of having adults who would listen to them, encourage them and help them to discern how they can be part of God's plan. For example, Eli helped Samuel to recognize the voice of God; without Eli's help in discernment, Samuel may not have realized it was God calling him (1 Sam. 3.8–9). David needed Samuel to discern that God wanted to appoint him as the next King of Israel (1 Sam. 16.10–13). Being equipped to discern God's voice and call is an important skill and gift that helps children to grow as they seek to live out their faith, and in so doing, bless the wider faith community. We also discovered the importance of fellowship in the body of Christ, where members share with each other to empower and enable all to share in the mission of God (e.g. Rom. 15.26; Gal. 2.9). These findings challenge and urge us to consider how children and young people are listened to and encouraged by adults to use their skills and gifts, and to partner with God and the wider church in the mission of God. If, as Powell, Mulder and Griffin suggest, young people are asking the question, 'What difference do I make?', then they should have the opportunity to discover their purpose within the body of Christ as they partake in building God's kingdom here on earth.[13]

The 'Growing Faith' report points to research that consistently shows that a key factor in the growth of faith in children is their 'active participation in worship' and 'connection to other adults in the faith community'.[14] The report also shows the contrast that many young people experience between participating in leadership, worship and decision-making in school, and the lack of opportunities to be involved in similar ways in their local church. The report argues that the level of engagement that children can experience within their school community 'needs to be replicated more often in children and young people's experience of church'.[15] Another report, based on research exploring what helps children and young people to stay 'rooted' in their faith and their local church, also found that children and young people value being seen as equal members of the body, and therefore hope to be given the same chances to lead and serve as adults have in the church community.[16] However, a multinational research project, surveying 207 churches across 18 nations in 2021, found that in 79 per cent of respondents 'children are not always involved in the church's mission', and only 16 per cent of churches described having 'an ethos of viewing children as disciples, active agents within the church and a sense of modelling and mentoring to support them in interacting more'.[17]

Our churches can no longer ignore the biblical examples of how God calls children to participate and be active in their faith, or the many voices of our children today which call out for their gifts to be used. There clearly needs to be change in our churches. Even among the rapidly growing number of books looking at the importance of children in church, there seems to be a lacuna when it comes to talking and writing about the vocation of children. We need to return to our first question in this book about how we view children. Perhaps, instead of asking children what they want to do when they 'grow up', we might ask them what they feel called to do *today*. What are the gifts and skills of our children and young people in church today? Inviting children to participate to include them in the mission and ministry of the church is wonderful, but doing so to help them to discern their gifts and how to use them is even better. If we can link their participation to their gifts and skills, to the discernment of their vocation now in the church, not just in the future, then their inclusion is not simply to help them stay in church but to empower them as agents of service and transformation, called by God. Furthermore, the gifts and ministry of our children and young people will bless the whole community, contributing to the spiritual formation and deepening of discipleship across all generations in the body of Christ. In their research, Powell, Mulder and Griffin found that when churches prioritize children and young people, all ages are edified, with one church member commenting: 'Young people are like salt. When they're included, they make everything taste better.'[18]

As such, we need to reflect on how we see children participating in our church, and why: what is our theological understanding of or motivation for their participation? It is perfectly valid for our motivation to include them in acts of service to be centred upon helping our children and young people to deepen their sense of identity, belonging and purpose. I would suggest this is where we need to start. If our church is one that would fall apart without its rotas, where possible and with regard to good safeguarding

## INTERGENERATIONAL WORSHIP, MINISTRY AND VOCATION

practice, let us invite our children to join them so they can turn some of the many cogs that make the machine of church whirr into action. Let us invite them on to the welcoming team, or the fundraising team, the eco-church team or to serve biscuits and cake at the coffee morning. Let's invite them to read in church or carry up the elements for communion.

However, there is a fine line between tokenism and genuine inclusion, and so while we invite our children and young people to participate, we must also intentionally and prayerfully be nurturing an environment where we, and they, can see their particular gifts and skills emerging and then discover how they can genuinely use these gifts. As Jaison writes: 'The participation of children takes intentionality and vision.'[19] We therefore move from helping children and young people to deepen their sense of identity and belonging to helping them discern their gifts and grow in confidence in how God has made them. The transition may not make any material change; a child may start out helping to serve the biscuits and continue to do so. The difference is that they start out essentially as an extra pair of hands, albeit a valuable pair, but they decide to continue in this role because they have discerned that they have the gift of hospitality in helping to foster a community of grace, skills in communicating and relating with others, and making people feel special when they receive that biscuit.

Sometimes it is a case of waiting, watching, praying and encouraging when the time is right. One of the young children in our congregation, Isla, used to be very shy in large crowds and would rarely detach herself from her mother's legs. One time, during our weekly evening communion service, I noticed her watching Ana (our chapel assistant) preparing the communion table. Isla suddenly jumped off her mother's lap and hurried closer to the front, where she continued to watch Ana from behind a pillar. Ana noticed and gestured to her, inviting her to come over. I watched, amazed, as Ana gently showed her what to do and together they set the communion table. Every week from that moment, Isla joined Ana for those few minutes of preparing the communion table while everyone sang the hymn. Some of us held our breath as Ana permitted her to carry the rather full chalice over to the table, which she did beautifully. Ana freely gave away her 'job' and assumed another role of encouraging this child; Isla in turn encouraged other children to serve in this way. I learned a lot from Ana. I admired how she had noticed Isla's curiosity and invited her closer, and how she did not divide the task between 'adult-only' tasks and safer 'child-friendly' tasks. I admired how she elevated Isla (and the other children who followed) so that they became equals in a team. I was grateful for how unperturbed Ana was on that first evening when, halfway through her task, she invited Isla to help. I pray we could have more Anas in our churches, and more Islas, who, when they find the courage and the curiosity, step up and joyfully serve, and in so doing, create a queue of eager children behind them.

In the previous chapter, I described how life-changing it was for me to start attending my local church when I was 15, where I found identity and belonging in an intergenerational community of care and support. However, it was also life-changing because it was while I found myself belonging to this beautiful community that I felt God calling me to be a vicar at the age of 16. At the time, life felt like I was on a conveyor belt: my grades suggested that I should follow a certain route, which for quite a few years I had been convinced by, but something had shifted inside and now I wanted to stop the conveyor. I knew God was calling me to jump off, which felt exciting but also terrifying. Jumping off meant freedom, but it also meant I would lose a sense of security in the predictability of the conveyor belt. However, a few members of the church independently encouraged me to think about being a vicar (even though I had not said anything about it to them). My mum mentioned it to one of the ministers, who in turn encouraged me to keep praying and put me in touch with someone outside that church to help me discern my sense of call. At every turn I was expecting people to laugh at me, but instead, I found encouragement. Most of all, I found it was the older people in church who really supported me and delighted in my faith and vocation.

Quite beautifully, several years later, I have just returned to this church as the Priest in Charge. It is profoundly moving to know that this is where I first heard God's call on my life as a child, and that he knew at the time that he would guide me back here one day. It is also profoundly moving to be the priest of some of those who were the first to encourage me in my faith and vocation. As I seek to nurture these saints, some of whom are now in their 80s and 90s, I remember that they were the ones who nurtured me as a child, and who prayed for my faith. I return to this church with passion and personal conviction for the nurturing of both our children and young people *and* our older brothers and sisters; for the growth of the church, and of faith, depends upon the mutual nurturing of faith and vocation across and among all our generations.

## Conclusion

Worship is at the heart of the church – of its purpose, its identity, its belonging and its story. Worship is at the heart of feasts, festivals, celebrations, anointings, commissioning, licensing and ordinations, as well as at the heart of tragedy, sorrow and lament. If we are passionate about the central place of worship in our church, then we should also be convinced that children and young people should be part of this worship. As Smit writes: 'If our children are to fully participate in the life of the church, they must participate meaningfully with all ages in worship.'[20] Additionally, worshipping together shapes everything else that flows out of worship:

> Intergenerational worship practices foster a sense of belonging for each generation and nurture spiritual connections and relationships across the generations. Ultimately, worshipping intergenerationally permeates the wider ministry of the church and shapes the entire culture of the church.[21]

If the body gathers for worship and children are not part of this worship space, then the culture of the church can quickly become an age-based culture in which plans, organization and decision-making are centred upon adults. If, however, worship is intergenerational and children and young people are not only seen worshipping but also enable it to happen in various ways, then the culture of the church becomes an intergenerational culture in which its mission and ministry genuinely include children and young people. Intergenerational worship leads to intergenerational ministry, where all generations come together 'in mutual serving, sharing, or learning within the core activities of the church in order to live out being the body of Christ to each other and the greater community'.[22] This, in turn, fosters an environment where children and teenagers can discern their own vocation. Their purpose in contributing to the ministry of the church is not only about helping them to feel rooted in their church but also about helping them to discern their gifts and how God might be calling them to use these gifts to edify the whole church and beyond into the wider community. Intergenerational worship and ministry enables all ages to encounter, and be transformed, called and equipped by God. In this way, the whole body grows in faith together, as all people grow closer in fellowship within the community of faith.

## Notes

1 H. C. Allen and C. Barnett, 2018, 'Addressing the two intergenerational questions', in H. C. Allen (ed.), *InterGenerate: Transforming Churches through Intergenerational Ministry*, Abilene, TX: Abilene Christian University Press, pp. 17–24, p. 17.

2 M. Volf, 2019, *Exclusion and Embrace: A Theological Exploration of Identity, Otherness, and Reconciliation*, Nashville, TN: Abingdon Press, p. 9.

3 N. Drake and B. Drake, 2021, *Worship for Everyone: Unlocking the Transforming Power of All-Age Worship*, London: SPCK, p. 16.

4 Drake and Drake, *Worship for Everyone*, pp. 23–4.

5 T. B. Smit, 'Five best intergenerational practices for small churches', in Allen, *InterGenerate*, pp. 131–9, p. 133.

6 J. H. Westerhoff, 2012, *Will Our Children Have Faith?*, third edition, New York: Morehouse Publishing, p. 59. For more on rituals and

young people, see K. Powell, J. Mulder and B. Griffin, 2016, *Growing Young: Six Essential Strategies to Help Young People Discover and Love Your Church*, Grand Rapids, MI: Baker Books, pp. 155–6.

7 H. C. Allen, C. Lawton, C. and C. L. Seibel, 2023, *Intergenerational Christian Formation: Bringing the Whole Church Together in Ministry, Community, and Worship*, Downers Grove, IL: InterVarsity Press, p. 173.

8 I am aware of the irony in saying this, since we have just been considering the importance of recognizing the different needs of different people. However, this has been in the wider context of trying to create a worship space that is not biased towards only one or two people groups, but that tries to reach out to different people, especially those who are not always seen or recognized in some of our 'main' services. Preferences and needs do matter, but when it comes to intergenerational worship, those who are able to flex and adapt should do so.

9 N. Shepherd, 2016, *Faith Generation: Retaining Young People and Growing the Church*, London: SPCK, p. 86.

10 Smit, 'Five best intergenerational practices for small churches', p. 133.

11 R. Nye, 2009, *Children's Spirituality: What It Is and Why It Matters*, London: Church House Publishing, p. 9.

12 L. Moore, 2016, *All-Age Worship*, second edition, Abingdon: The Bible Reading Fellowship, p. 57.

13 Powell, Mulder and Griffin, *Growing Young*, p. 95.

14 D. Clinton, N. Genders and D. Male, 2019, 'Growing Faith: Churches, Schools and Households' (GS 2121), General Synod of the Church of England, The Archbishops' Council, p. 3.

15 Clinton, Genders and Male, 'Growing Faith: Churches, Schools and Households', p. 6.

16 Church of England Education Office, 2016, 'Rooted in the Church: Summary Report', Research by Design.

17 S. Holmes, L. Murray, M. Larson, S. Price, P. Whitehead and V. de Abreu, 2022, 'Do church structures enable children's and family ministry to grow? A multinational research project', *Nurturing Young Faith*, 1 November, p. 9, https://www.nurturingyoungfaith.org/post/full-report-do-church-structures-encourage-children-family-ministry, accessed 12.01.2025.

18 Powell, Mulder and Griffin, *Growing Young*, p. 203.

19 J. Jaison, 2022, 'Affirming children's dignity as a theological vision and mandate', in R. Tan, N. A. Patellar and L. A. Hefford (eds), *God's Heart for Children: Practical Theology from Global Perspectives*, Carlisle: Langham Global Library, pp. 13–24, p. 21.

20 Smit, 'Five best intergenerational practices for small churches', p. 133.

21 Allen, Lawton and Seibel, *Intergenerational Christian Formation*, p. 189.
22 Allen, Lawton and Seibel, *Intergenerational Christian Formation*, p. 18.

# 6

# Households: Encountering Faith Together

### SARAH STRAND

Praying with children is one of my favourite things to do and it has been my total joy and privilege to pray with my own children every day since they were born. Sometimes this looks like a snatched, 'thank you Jesus for today, help us sleep well tonight' kind of prayer, sometimes it has been prayer led and initiated by them, which could be silly or serious, sometimes it has involved each of us responding to deep joy, enormous challenges or the mundane reality of everyday life. I am always surprised (even though I really shouldn't be!) by the depth and the beauty of prayers I have been privileged to hear and share with children, even by the youngest of pray-ers. At the age of four, my eldest son prayed, 'Thank you God for the joy-ness you have. Come in.' I made a note of this at the time and it serves as a reminder to me of how precious it is to grow together in faith in our families and households.

## The nature of family and household

There are 168 hours in a week (some of us might wish that there were more!). On average in the UK, children spend about 32 of those hours every week at school (based on a standard six-hour school day). If the family attends church, they might spend anything between two to six hours in church-based activities (including Sunday school, activities or clubs). This leaves a whole 130 hours each week that they will spend at home, sleeping, eating, playing, chatting, or outside their home or in wrap-around care, in clubs, leisure or other activities with family, carers and friends. When I talk to families about faith in their households, lots of parents and carers have told me that they struggle with time and with confidence, among lots of other things we will discuss in this chapter. Many have said to me that school or church is the place where their child receives the best input or discipleship of their faith. But a child's time outside school and church far outweighs the time they spend there. Parents and carers know their children the best and are in the best position to disciple and nurture faith in their own households – with more time and opportunity than they might realize.

This chapter will explore a theology of family and household faith, drawing on themes from the Old and New Testaments as well as some key theologians. We will also explore some research into family life today alongside some common challenges and concerns families can have as they seek to nurture faith in their households. This chapter will not give all the practical answers but I hope it will open up a conversation, offer some theological resources and raise some questions as we reflect on what it means to support family faith in households.

Whether you are a parent or carer, a church leader, a youth or children's minister, a volunteer, an educator or anyone in between, I hope this chapter will raise some questions, explore some challenges and give you some resources and hope for the future. Within it, we will explore what a theology of family and household might look like and how our understanding of both theology and practice can shape how we support the faith within households.

## Household faith

The church has been wrestling for centuries with questions about how to develop, nurture or grow faith within families. As we will explore, there is a clear sense of how faith was passed on within households in the Bible, but over the centuries many theologians have wrestled with the questions about how best to shape and influence the faith of the next generation. Martin Luther, in his attempt to make faith accessible to children and families produced one of the first ever children's Bibles in 1529 with his *Passional*, which combined illustrations with stories from the Old Testament and the life of Jesus.[1] Written in German, it was designed to be accessible to lay people and children and demonstrated Luther's commitment to the discipleship of children within the home. Luther began a legacy which has led to hundreds of thousands of Bible translations, storybooks and resources to educate and nurture children's faith.

Throughout the centuries, the church has long held a role in children's education. The Church of England has played a significant role in this, through its programme of education and the development of the Sunday School Movement in the late eighteenth century. Alongside substantial cultural and societal shifts in the late nineteenth and twentieth centuries, including declining church attendance, this education movement led to an increasing 'professionalization' of children's faith and religious education. As a consequence, families came to increasingly rely on the church or school to engage in the work of discipleship and passing on faith. This is a trend which has only accelerated in the last 30 years. Ruth Worsley recognizes a 'growing vacuum' in household faith and the passing-on of faith through home relationships.[2] It is possible to argue that out of the three spaces of church, home and school, home is often considered to be the 'weakest' in terms of growing together in faith, as well as the most under-researched. Schools (particularly church schools) have intentional, timetabled time to engage with issues of faith and spirituality. Our churches might not have any children attending, or they might have a brilliant and full children and youth ministry programme but even if children are just turning up on a Sunday with no other provision, they are listening to Scripture, hearing prayers and experiencing something of what the body of Christ looks like. However, the picture can be quite mixed in households. Many families and households are thinking and praying carefully about what it means to walk alongside their children in faith. However, in my own research I have found parents are often bewildered, lacking in confidence in their own faith and theology and on top of that, are battling with the stressful and complex demands of twenty-first-century parenting. Developing household faith can be added to an already long list of 'shoulds' in an already over-burdened, guilt-ridden and expectation-laden landscape of family life.

## Family life today

What is it like to raise a family in the twenty-first century? What are the pressures, the joys and the challenges facing families, children and young people today? Working patterns, the cost of childcare, the abundance and pressure of extra-curricular activities, financial concerns and the cost of living, the impact of technology, the internet and social media, mental health crises, confidence, a lack of support, under-resourced and under-funded education systems, global political instability, war, trafficking and sexual exploitation, violence. I imagine you could add many more things to this list. According to the Children's Society, in 2021 4.3 million children were living in poverty in the UK, which accounts for almost one third of all children.[3] Writing from the context of north-east England, I'm deeply conscious of the impact of the cost-of-living crisis, global financial instability and localized child poverty for those raising families in my local area. I'm also conscious of the impact of global factors which are impacting children and families in countries across the world in unprecedented ways.

Families are more scheduled, pressured and complicated than ever before. For those families who have the privilege of financial resources, there are more clubs, activities and opportunities than ever before. But family life, patterns and expectations are also changing quickly. Family circumstances are often complex and potentially involve blended families, single-parent families or a whole host of other family patterns. Changes in childcare provision and funding, patterns of living and both the cost and availability of housing are also impacting family lives. In short, families are under more pressure and facing more challenges than ever before. This will be a picture that many of us are already very familiar with, but how does our theology offer insight into this tumultuous, fast-changing and challenging reality?

## Family and household in the Old Testament

When you think of a household today what picture immediately comes into your mind?

Perhaps it is a neat, pretty house with a white picket fence, a rose garden and four happy, smiling faces? Perhaps it's a terraced house with a red door and two small faces looking out of a window? Perhaps it's a tower block, a mansion or something else entirely? What does the family look like? And what might that tell you about the way you have been shaped to think about households today?

What it means to be a household has changed and developed dramatically over the centuries. In the Old Testament, a household was seen as a 'residential extended family'[4] which, while spanning several generations, included servants, enslaved people and other dependants. Family communities were grown through birth, family ties, kinship, marriage and covenants. Israelite families functioned as independent, self-governing units economically, socially and judicially, in contrast to other ancient Near Eastern societies and in even starker contrast to the individual households we see in twenty-first-century Western life. While today children are viewed as a distinct demographic, particularly in economic and market terms, children in the Old Testament were viewed as an important part of a larger social and liturgical community.[5] Israelite families ate together, worshipped together, engaged in ritual and cultural customs together, often worked together and supported each other as a smaller community within a much larger religious community. The family also had an important theological function as '*beth 'ab*' or the 'household of God', which was the centre of theological and religious practice.[6] There are many places within the Old Testament, but particularly in Deuteronomy, Exodus and Proverbs, in which the outlines and expectations of family life and the passing on of faith within that communal, family household were explored. There were expectations on the behaviour and actions of both parents and children and all of it held together within a broader theological understanding of what it means to be God's chosen people, in covenant relationship with him.

Deuteronomy 11.18–21 makes clear the importance of the whole family understanding and remaining faithful to the commandments: 'Teach them to your children, talking about them when you are at home and when you are away, when you lie down and when you rise.' In Deuteronomy 29, all the family including outsiders were present at the renewing of the covenant and there are several places in Deuteronomy, including chapter 6, where the role of the family in passing on faith to the next generation is emphasized. There is also a strong theme in Proverbs of the theological role of the family in reading and teaching the stories of God through the generations. Proverbs 1.8–9 exhorts children to hear the instructions of their parents, while Proverbs 4.1–5 recalls the way teaching was passed between generations.

Sharing the stories of Scripture, whether in formal settings or at home, as outlined in Deuteronomy 11.19, would have formed an important part of this education. Patrick D. Miller argues that while it may be assumed that there were schools for instruction, 'the whole orientation of Deuteronomy is toward teaching in the family context.'[7] This teaching would have taken the form of daily recitation of the law, speaking and meditating on the law and the family participating in the religious life of the community.[8] The community would also have heard the whole law recited every seven years as a requirement (Deut. 31.10–13) and this reading would have reinforced the stories and law for the whole community as well as introducing younger children to them for the first time.

Sharing Bible stories at home and within families is one of the most important aspects of household faith we can encourage. Families often lack both confidence and resources in doing this, so purchasing Bibles and storybooks, recommending podcasts, supporting literacy and reading in school contexts and encouraging conversations around faith and storytelling are just a few small things which can support families to grow together in faith.

## It takes a village

Earlier in this chapter, I briefly explored the complexity and challenges of twenty-first-century parenting and family life and I raised the question of what pictures of family life we hold in our minds. We are hopefully all aware that families do not come in a neat, two-parents-and-two-children picture of nuclear family perfection. Families are grown, joined, merged, grown through adoption, fostering, fertility treatment, blending and so many other things besides. However, many of us still hold a picture in our minds of a family or a household as a nuclear family; two parents and two children. The sense of the family as a household, a community, in the Old Testament is very far removed from that very particular image of the nuclear family. Family in the Old Testament was much bigger than just two parents and two children. It was complex, extended, messy and, by almost all accounts, dysfunctional!

'It takes a village to raise a child' is an old proverb which has gained traction and publicity in recent years. It has trended regularly on social media and there is an encouragement for parents (often, in this case, mums) to find their 'village' or their 'tribe' in order to better raise their family and find the support they need both practically and emotionally. There's a sense in which parents are recognizing that they need the support, love, practical care and help from a broader community than simply their own family, whatever form it takes. With families moving away from traditional support networks, in some cases for work, affordability or housing or practicalities or simply struggling with the practical realities of daily life, parents are recognizing they are in greater need of the help and support which in previous generations may well have been on their doorstep.

The desire to 'find a village' does seem to reflect the Old Testament, communal approach to family life. But it is an easy statement to make without recognizing the challenges in developing a community or 'village' within a culture which still idolizes and prioritizes the nuclear family (as unrealistic as that may be) and in which economic, cultural and social factors often leave families isolated regardless. While many families do have strong networks of support and input, lots don't, and it can be a real challenge to discover and establish such a community. So how can we find a 'village' or support the households and families around us to build or discover one? The church seems like an ideal place to find an intergenerational community of love and practical, emotional and spiritual support.

## Creating community

The narratives around faith in the household have often focused particularly on the role of parents and have reinforced the nuclear family emphasis. But what if we used the understanding of *beth 'ab* and the theological vision for household faith to broaden our definition of what a family and a household is? The *Faith in the Nexus* research showed the importance of household networks in growing faith – including grandparents, godparents and others.[9] Supporting families with meaningful and deep relationships can play a really significant role in encouraging faith not just in children and young people but in the family as a whole. Grandparents (or surrogate grandparents if grandparents live at a distance) can play a particularly important role, often because they are involved in childcare, school pick-ups or are more available to children to talk. Grandparents are also more likely to have purchased a Bible or have had some connections with the local church, even if very loosely through marriage, baptisms or attendance at funerals. The *Faith in the Nexus* report also identified that faith-talk among siblings, as well as grandparents, was more common for many children than faith-talk with parents.[10] One of the most beautiful gifts to our own family, particularly as a clergy family who have moved between different locations, has been those from older generations who have loved us and our children. The offers of babysitting or support with school runs, the help with a rambunctious toddler, the ability to text in an emergency or to cry on the other end of a phone, the prayers offered, the relationships with growing children formed and cherished.

In an increasingly individualized society it is profoundly countercultural to build relationships beyond family and blood ties. To love and support not just a child or an adult, but an entire family. The intergenerational, beautiful body of Christ is well equipped for this ministry – with all the important caveats of appropriate boundaries, attention to safeguarding and honest conversations about hopes, needs and desires. We're able to support the growth of faith within households when we grow the full, diverse and beautiful *beth 'ab*, household of God.

## Family and household in the New Testament

The families of the Old Testament were often dysfunctional and problematic, although, as we've explored, the theological vision of the 'household of God' is clear. Within the New Testament, family and household life are explored within the Gospels as Jesus refers to the disruption of family relationships in Matthew 19.29, Mark 10.29–30 and Luke 18.29–30. We also see family dynamics within the Disciples, in Jesus' relationship with Martha, Mary and Lazarus and in the developing story of the life of the early church through the epistles. Perhaps the most well-known New Testament explorations of family life come within the 'Household Codes'[11] which explore the expectations for parent and child conduct, behaviour, discipline and expectations. In similar ways to the Old Testament, the New Testament does not offer an understanding of children as a distinct demographic, rather they are considered as part of a family unit which continues to have a theological and social function. But, contrary to the arguments of some historians, children still had an important place within family life. Judith Gundry-Wolf argues that there is strong evidence in the New Testament that children are disciples in their own right and she talks about five key characteristics of child disciples. First, children are the 'intended recipients of the reign of God',[12] referring to Jesus' blessing of the children in Mark 10.15. There has been a long debate about what Jesus' words and actions in this passage mean, but if we look to the Beatitudes, we see that Jesus offers blessing for the poor, the hungry, the grieving and the suffering and children also fit within those categories – vulnerable and powerless as they are. And it is that vulnerability and powerlessness which lies at the heart of Jesus extending the kingdom of God, and his own Kingship, to them.

Gundry-Wolf also identifies that children are trusting and dependent on God's mercy (Matt. 18.1–5), humble (Mark 9.33–37), representatives of Christ (Mark 9.30–33) and in unmediated relationship with Jesus (Eph. 6.1).[13] This is a set of characteristics and markers of discipleship which offer a foundation for prioritizing children as disciples. Children are disciples in their own right, in unmediated, full relationship with Jesus, but that is within the context of families and communities. There is very little romance or idealism within these biblical images of family, household and community life but it can be challenging, certainly in twenty-first-century western society, to relate to and recognize the social and theological functions of family life which is so drastically different from our own.

Recognizing children as disciples is an important step in releasing parents from guilt-driven parenting. God is already in relationship with children, right from the very beginning of their lives, and that relationship will continue. While we can support and enhance that relationship as parents, carers and leaders, showing with our lives, in our conversation and our decision-making what our Christian faith means – we are not responsible ultimately for their own relationship with Jesus.

## Intention for open-mindedness

The *Faith in the Nexus* report identified that one of the challenges highlighted particularly by parents, including parents who described themselves as Christian, was that they wanted to be open-minded and enable their children to make up their own minds about faith.[14] This is part of a trend in twenty-first-century parenting to empower children to make their own choices, be secure in their feelings and communicate their own needs. Many of these hopes and desires are positive and it is significant to empower and listen carefully to the voices of children and young people. However, this intention towards open-mindedness is a hallmark of an increasingly individualistic society and *Faith in the Nexus* notes:

> The expectation that a young child can construct their own identity does not take account of the need for the critical skill to evaluate the blocks, the parts, the threads needed to weave such an identity. Nor does it account for how independently an individual might be able to choose freely among other influencing factors.[15]

This is a really significant insight into contemporary culture and modern-day parenting. Lots of families, in choosing to 'let children decide for themselves', are making an active choice in the opposite direction. To be very clear, this is not an argument for the indoctrination of children or teenagers, or for the diminishing of their voice or perspective. But it is to make clear that an open-minded approach can often simply shape a child, or a family, in a different direction rather than genuinely offering a framework for free choice and exploration. Exploring faith together, asking the difficult questions, not being afraid to sit with doubt and uncertainty, enabling conversation and criticality, reading the Bible together and living out Christian discipleship in community (in all its messy reality) is much more likely to empower and enable a child to own their own relationship with God and their faith journey.

## A challenge for church leaders

The Covid-19 pandemic has left a lasting legacy for all of us. Children and young people at key times of transition and education were impacted deeply, alongside families who were wrestling with home schooling, health, employment and financial concerns. In the wake of Covid-19, research was commissioned in 2022 to explore the place of families in church post-Covid. Families reported that while the faith in their household had generally improved through the pandemic, at the same time their connections and engagement with the local church had been reduced.[16] Families were often creative and deeply committed to growing together in faith and discipleship at home during this time but there was a range of perceptions of how well these endeavours were supported by churches. The research discovered that

> a quarter of church leaders acknowledged that they did not know if the families in their church felt supported with nurturing faith at home and 51% of the families said that they did not feel supported or resourced with this by their local church.[17]

Parents, carers and church leaders were all in agreement about the best ways to nurture children's faith and it was clear that all parties thought that church and families should work closely together on this. However, while this perspective was clear, this was not what was reported as the reality of ministry among children and families. There seems to be a widening gap in understanding between the hopes, desires and perspectives of parents and families and those of church leaders. Half of the church leaders interviewed reported a 'need of parents to change how they engaged with faith, often conveying deficiencies in the personal faith of parents or their commitment to nurturing their child's faith'.[18] Church leaders are stating this while not indicating a desire to listen or engage with parents and families about their own perspectives on the challenges and joys of growing in faith together in households. While church leaders were critical of parents, they reported needing more volunteers, resources and time to give to events, services and activities. In deep contrast, Christian parents reported a desire for more 'personal, targeted and relational support from their local church for faith at home'.[19] This reinforces the theological discussion of *beth 'ab,* and the practical outcome of building relationship and community to support family household faith. The particular challenge here for church leaders is for deeper listening. It is easy to criticize parents from a distance, without having understood the unique perspectives, challenges and joys of parenting for faith in households today. However, there is also freedom that families don't necessarily want more activities and events – but rather relationship, personal connection and developing community.

What we have here is a complex picture; some parents think it is their responsibility to share faith with their children but aren't reading the Bible in the home and aren't talking to their children about faith. But there are other families in which faith in the home was strengthened through the challenges of the last few years but who have discovered a big disconnect between faith in the home and church. The key response here I think must be listening. There is not a one-size-fits-all, 'here is how you should approach' growing faith in households (just in the same way that there isn't a one-size-fits-all approach to parenting) – not for parents, and certainly not for churches and church leaders. Building relationships and listening to the reality of where families are with faith must be the starting point!

## What about households and families in which parents do not have Christian faith?

So far, this chapter has focused on families who already have some kind of foundation of faith – however that is being expressed or practised within the home. We are, of course, in a culture in which there are many more families without faith, without the influence of a church school and with very limited, if any, engagement with church. When it comes to building and supporting faith with those families, I think the principles remain the same. Starting from a perspective of listening and understanding, rather than a distant judgement. Community and faith are built when lives are shared together. When children or young people are attending groups or activities without parents, what would it look like to build relationships, engage in active listening and seeking understanding of the context of their family life? What would it look like to care for whole families, to give time, energy and prayer? This is an activity which does require time, energy and love alongside good boundaries and accountability. It is also an activity which will be best shared across the church and not just with the church leaders. Why not start a conversation with the children, young people and families in your community today?

## Notes

1 Ruth B. Bottigheimer, 1996, *The Bible for Children: From the Age of Gutenberg to the Present*, Grand Rapids, MI, Yale University Press, p. 23.

2 Ruth Worsley, 2020, foreword in H. Worsley, *How Not to Totally Put Your Children Off God*, Oxford: Lion Hudson, p. 6.

3 The Children's Society, n.d., https://www.childrenssociety.org.uk/what-we-do/our-work/ending-child-poverty, accessed 07.03.2025.

4 Peter Pothen, 1992, *Unpacking the Family*, Grove Ethical Studies No. 87, Nottingham: Grove Books, p. 5.

5 Matthews McGinnis, Claire R., 2008, 'Exodus as a "Text of Terror" for Children', in Marcia J. Bunge (ed.), *The Child in the Bible*, Grand Rapids, MI: Eerdmans: p. 25.

6 Pothen, *Unpacking the Family*, p. 5.

7 Patrick D. Miller, 2008, 'That the children may know: children in Deuteronomy' in Bunge, *The Child in the Bible*, p. 54.

8 Miller, 'That the children may know: children in Deuteronomy', p. 54.

9 A. Casson, S. Hulbert, M. Woolley and B. Bowie, 2020, *Faith in the Nexus: Church Schools and Children's Exploration of Faith in the Home: A NICER Research Study of Twenty Church Primary Schools in England*, Canterbury: Canterbury Christ Church University.

10 Casson et al., *Faith in the Nexus*, p. 30.

## HOUSEHOLDS

11 Household codes can be found in Ephesians 5.22—6.9; Colossians 3.18—4.1 as well as 1 Timothy 2, Titus and 1 Peter.

12 Judith M. Gundry-Wolf, 2001, 'The least and the greatest: children in the New Testament' in Marcia J. Bunge (ed.), *The Child in Christian Thought*, Grand Rapids, MI: Eerdmans, p. 37.

13 Gundry-Wolf, 'The least and the greatest: children in the New Testament', pp. 38–56.

14 Casson et al., *Faith in the Nexus*, p. 31.

15 Casson et al., *Faith in the Nexus*, p. 32.

16 Sarah Holmes, A. Casson, Richard Powney, et al., 2022, 'What is the place of families in church post-Covid?', https://www.nurturingyoungfaith.org/post/research-report-what-is-the-place-of-families-in-church-post-covid, accessed 28.02.2025.

17 Holmes, 'What is the place of families in church post-Covid?', p. 3.

18 Holmes, 'What is the place of families in church post-Covid?', p. 3.

19 Holmes, 'What is the place of families in church post-Covid?', p. 3.

# 7

# School Communities: Listening to the Voices of Children and Teenagers

## SARAH STRAND

In 2023, Cranmer Hall, part of St John's College in Durham University, partnered with the Growing Faith Foundation to develop a dedicated research and training centre exploring the foundational theological questions which lie behind so much of what we can see happening in the churches around us. We had witnessed declining numbers, many churches with no children or young people at all and as a result we wanted to explore two key questions:

1. Why is ministry and mission with children and young people not happening?
2. Why should ministry and mission with children and young people be happening?

Anecdotally, we had seen so many churches across the Church of England and other denominations who were struggling to work with, engage and prioritize children and young people. We also felt strongly that the 'Why should it be happening?' question is often neglected, particularly in relation to academic theological enquiry in this area. We wanted to delve into these questions deeply and, with a small team, we spent time listening to the voices of children and young people in both primary and secondary schools as well as parents, teaching staff, education leaders and church leaders. This research project sought specifically to listen to children and young people within a school context and to draw explicitly on their experience and understanding of faith, reading the Bible and prayer both in school and at home. It was crucial for us to engage with a diversity of voices, not just with those children and young people who can be found within church settings.

This initially small research project expanded into a large one, as we engaged with over 400 children and young people from two Church of England primary schools and two Church of England secondary schools in the north-east. The four schools were in very different locations and were not connected by feeder relationships. Each of these school contexts draws pupils from a range of contexts and backgrounds and many will not have a Christian faith, even though they attend a school with a faith perspective. The age range we covered within the research was from 4 to 16, with a cross section of children from diverse geographical and socio-economic contexts. The research was conducted in small focus groups, with groups of no more than ten students gathered together to discuss a set of ten questions, with an additional two questions added for the secondary school age bracket. Children were given a brief that there were no right or wrong answers, but rather an opportunity to discuss their thoughts and ideas with the researchers. We were blown away by the responses we received from the children and young people and this chapter is dedicated to them. We want their voices to be heard and for that to continue to shape our research, thinking, reflections, practice and ministry.[1]

## Who is God?

All children were asked who they thought God was and there was a very interesting and noticeable trend in the responses the children gave. For those in Reception and Year 1, Jesus was the most popular answer about who God is, with one child commenting, 'God is the son of God who helps everybody and helps us to make better choices.' God as creator was also a popular answer with children in Year 1, who responded in equal numbers that God was either Jesus or God's Son or a creator. Children had also begun to identify God by relationships within this year group, recognizing God as 'Mary and Joseph's son' or 'baby Jesus'. From Year 2 God as creator became the most popular answer and the number of 'Jesus' related responses dramatically decreased. Year 2 pupils reflected on God as 'in charge of the whole entire world' or 'the person who created the world'. The popularity of God as creator in the responses continued to climb from Year 2, to Years 3, 4, 5 and 6. By Year 6, 50 per cent of the children interviewed responded that God was a creator, although the diversity of other answers also increased. Children described God as 'creator and saviour', as the 'person who invented the world' and 'the king of heaven'. Answers by Year 6 tended to be more abstract and increasing in complexity, in line with understandings of child development. The response of God as creator peaked in popularity in Year 7 with 60 per cent of children answering in this way. It is interesting to reflect on why this might be and whether the school curriculum and particularly the emphasis on creation care may be influencing the way children respond to this question. What is clear is that, while there was a diversity of responses, there were some clear and consistent themes and understandings of God which the children had developed over time.

While children in Year 7 had a strong understanding of God as creator, the prevalence of this answer decreased dramatically throughout the secondary school age bracket. By Year 8, the young people responding began to identify whether they believed in God or not as they responded to the question. The proportion of self-identifying 'non-believers' increased through the age brackets from 18 per cent in Year 9, to 24 per cent in Year 10 and 22 per cent in Year 11. There may be a number of factors behind this trend including being in a group setting with their peers, increasing confidence levels in sharing what they think and changing relationships with authority figures. It also fits understandings within faith and adolescent development as the teenage years open up opportunities for questioning and challenging previously held assumptions. However, there was still a very strong trend of young people associating God most predominantly with the role of creator. One Year 10 pupil described God: 'He's just like some man who rules the world or something. He'd probably be like proper nice if you met him but you'd have to understand him though.'

## God and primary school values

The primary school children (aged 4–11) were asked a supplementary question, 'What would God be like if you met him?' The responses to this question overwhelmingly categorized God as friendly, kind and compassionate. A number of the responses directly reflected the values of the school they attended, and this was articulated explicitly by some of the children, particularly in the older age groups. It's interesting to reflect on the influence of school values and vision statements within faith and theological formation in Church of England schools. While the vision statements are important, they can reflect generally positive moralistic attributes which are transferred to a child's understanding of God and Christian faith, sometimes with limited opportunity for critical engagement and nuance.

For those in reception, God was someone who 'helps other people' and who would 'say hello to you'. Answers in Year 1 began to become slightly more abstract; while the majority referenced kindness and friendliness, several children described physical aspects of God's appearance, describing his beard or 'yellow clothes 'cause he's the light'. Gentle, peaceful, friendly and nice were the attributes most popular in Year 2, while in Year 3 God's caring nature was emphasized – 'He'd say, are you OK?' – as well as that God is 'invisible'. Mirroring the answers to the first question, children in Year 4 had a strong emphasis on creation: 'He made all of these beautiful people.' Responses in Year 5 and Year 6 were often qualified by a statement at the beginning like 'I imagine', 'I picture' or 'I would describe' with one Year 5 pupil responding: 'I imagine God as someone who is thankful for everything and he would tell you if you were being not very kind.' The Year 6 responses again focused on positive attributes to God but also became more abstract, with one pupil describing God as 'very posh' and the physical descriptions of God continued including 'God is kind and tall' and 'floating'.

Generally, the children were confident in answering these first two questions and had quite firmly established ideas of who God is and what he is like. The responses were beautifully diverse and revealed quite a wide spectrum of understanding, from some more conventional theological responses to others which would be outside the usual expectations of Christian theology. The school values had a strong influence on how children viewed and understood who God is and there is some important learning within that for schools to reflect on the images of God they are teaching and reinforcing. What qualities and attributes are being left out? Where, if any, are the gaps? What is the influence of the school curriculum on this (particularly in relation to God as creator)? And how can children have the space to discuss, to question and to wonder as they explore together God's identity?

## Engaging with Scripture in primary schools

Children in all age categories were asked four questions about the Bible. First, 'What is the Bible?' which sought to explore what they understood about the Bible, alongside what and who it was for. Second, a question exploring their knowledge and understanding of Bible stories and which stories stood out for them. Third, a question exploring what they liked about the Bible and finally, what they didn't like or found difficult about the Bible.

Throughout the primary-school-age groups, the children had a secure understanding of the Bible as a book which was connected to stories about Jesus and/or God. In Reception, there was a high proportion of children who weren't sure of their answer, with over 44 per cent answering with a variety of 'don't know'. Although some were able to connect their answers with

'God and his friends' and 'the story of the Son of God'. The proportion of 'don't know' in Year 1 was still high, with 39 per cent of the children responding in this way. Children from Year 2 onward seemed to have a more secure understanding with over 62 per cent making connections between the Bible as a storybook which connected with Jesus and God. Within this age group, connections began to be made again with school values, with one child describing 'the Bible is about Jesus using all the values'. The significance of reality and fantasy in children's development was also emphasized from Year 2 onward, with a child describing the Bible as 'a special book that tells us about real stories and real people'.

From Year 3 onward the percentage of children making connections with the Bible, stories and Jesus and God became increasingly higher, from 64 per cent in Year 3 to a very significant 97 per cent in Year 6. However, in Years 5 and 6 there was a high volume of answers which described the Bible simply as a 'holy book' or a 'book for Christians' and the moralistic or teaching aspects of the Bible were emphasized more: 'The Bible is a book about how Christians should behave' (Year 4 pupil) and 'The Bible is the book of stories that God taught to people to teach us lessons' (Year 6 pupil). The progression from storytelling in the Early Years, to special stories connecting with school values within Years 2–4 and moving on to teaching and moralistic outcomes in Years 5 and 6 may again reflect the current curriculum and approach to teaching the Bible within schools, and church schools in particular, but also its place and role within collective worship.

Children across the primary year groups were aware of a wide range of Bible stories from both the Old and New Testaments. Popular choices from the Old Testament included the creation story, Adam and Eve, Noah, Moses, Joseph and David and Goliath. Notable stories from the New Testament were Jesus' life, death and resurrection, including specifically the Christmas story, the Last Supper, Jesus' miracles, Jesus calming the storm and the parables. It was clear that children had been exposed to quite a broad and varied range of stories, which was encouraging.

Additionally, the influence of the school values again emerged as a strong theme, with a child from Year 2 commenting, 'All our school values have stories to go with them.' It is fantastic that children have the opportunity to engage with Bible stories both in lessons and worship in church school contexts, but it is also worth reflecting on the framework which may need to be provided to ensure that space is given to explore Bible stories separately from this framework. Space to wonder, question and discover more is so important as children develop both their literary and faith landscapes. Offering explicit connections between Bible stories and either values or moralistic outcomes can be restrictive and reduce the potential and opportunities stories provide from educational, theological and spiritual perspectives.

When it came to exploring with the primary school children what they liked and didn't like about the Bible there were a wide range of answers which were often very specific, reflecting on particular stories which they loved hearing or the physical act of reading – including one child who described that they didn't like the 'thin paper' of the Bible they had read and a number of others who named the long words, its complexity and the fact that they didn't really enjoy reading in general. However, the most striking thing among these responses was the sheer volume of children across all age groups who named Jesus' death as the thing they didn't like. Over a third of all the children involved in the research named Jesus' death in this way and it was a particularly noticeable trend among Key Stage One children. It is perhaps easy to see why; Jesus' death is violent, sad and challenging and stands in contrast to some of the Bible stories the children named and enjoyed the most. It can also be difficult for children to understand aspects of the story, particularly if it is separated from the rest of the biblical story when it is explored. The crucifixion, and indeed the entire story of Jesus' betrayal and death, is really important to share with children but these responses emphasize the care which needs to be taken alongside the space for processing children may need as they wonder and explore.

In the light of these findings it may be helpful to reflect on engagement with the Bible in school contexts: do teaching and support staff have confidence in handling and discussing the Bible? Is there space for critical engagement and questioning for both children and adults? How can the Bible be used within worship in addition to communicating about school values? What do creative approaches to storytelling look like within that and what is realistic within an already busy and demanding school context? How do we deal well with the darker and more challenging parts of the Bible? And what does it mean to support children in doing so?

## Engaging with Scripture in secondary schools

Pupils in the secondary schools confidently described the Bible in four key ways: as a holy book for Christians, as a book of instructions Christians follow, as teaching or direction for life and, finally, as words from God. There was a range of responses across the year groups but almost all could be categorized into those four perspectives. It was clear that a minority of pupils within the focus groups professed Christian faith but most did not. When reflecting on the further questions about what stood out for them in the Bible, what they liked and what they didn't like, there were some common themes. First, the significance of the gift of a Bible or access to a Bible at home. Pupils in both Years 7 and 8 reflected on reading Bibles which had been given to them in primary school as they made the transition to secondary school:

> I think I have a little Bible at home that I got given in assembly. I think my mum used to have a Bible as well so sometimes I used to read it to see what was in there and if it can help me to answer any of my questions. (Year 7)

> I like the Bible because ... so one time I read a piece of it because I got given a Bible in year six so then I read a piece of it and [thought it would be a] bit boring but actually it weren't boring. I don't mind it because it helps Christians get through life and it inspires people to do more. (Year 8)

These stories reinforce the significance of enabling children to access a Bible at key points of transition, but particularly in Year 6 as they move to secondary school. Whether gifted by school or by church, this is an important opportunity for children to have access to the Bible to support their explorations of faith. If children don't attend a church school, it is still worth exploring whether a gift from a local church to a community primary school would be welcome, alongside reflecting on how to resource children and young people to continue to explore faith through the Bible for themselves.

There are echoes among the secondary school pupils of the emphasis placed on school values shared by the primary school pupils, with a Year 8 pupil reflecting that the Bible 'teaches you to be resilient'. The impact of school vision and values remains a strong theme, which positively identifies how well established and integrated staff and students at the schools we engaged with were in their vision and values. However, it also presents challenges: what does it look like for young people to engage with the Bible outside a moralistic or 'value' based perspective? How can the full breadth of the Bible be explored and where can there be further opportunities for nuance and complexity?

Secondary school pupils were very vocal about what they didn't like about the Bible, with an overwhelming number of responses identifying that the Bible was too long, the language was too challenging, or it was boring. One Year 8 pupil stated that their challenges with the Bible could be found in its complexity: 'I don't like it 'cause it tries to make you see the truth it doesn't just straight up tell you what it means, you have to think about it really hard.'

It could be argued that this level of challenge isn't necessarily a bad thing! But the perception of inaccessibility and confusion is important to acknowledge. There was also noticeable wrestling with the 'traditional' opinions of the Bible not connecting with modern day perspectives and several students explicitly referenced what the Bible says about sexuality as something which presented a challenge for them. Questions about creation and what was 'real' were raised in almost all year groups, with Year

11 pupils raising some very specific points: 'God made everything but there's no mention of dinosaurs, that's what I don't understand.'

What was clear throughout was that many of the young people were asking big questions, were wrestling with big theological concepts and were wondering about important life issues including suffering, the relationship between science and faith, sexuality, creation and justice, to name just a few. Offering a forum for secondary school pupils to address and explore these questions in an open and judgement-free space seems like something which could be really significant here. This is something specific the local church could offer support with. What would it look like for churches to offer space within school for discussion and conversation? How can children and young people be supported to question and explore? In what ways can supportive relationships be built for both students and staff?

The final section of this chapter will explore the incredible range of questions the children and young people shared with our researchers. They aren't necessarily questions which need to be answered directly but they reveal an incredible curiosity and a desire to know more which should be encouraged and explored.

## Engaging in prayer: uniting church, home and school

All the primary school children were asked a very simple question: Do you pray? Along with a supplementary question about where, how and when they pray. Out of the total of 211 primary school pupils who were interviewed, 184 of them said that they prayed, while 21 said that they didn't and just six replied that they weren't sure. This is an amazing indicator that children's spiritual lives are deeper and more connected to God than we initially anticipated they might be. Their prayer lives are also not restricted to one location or context; pupils across all year groups identified praying in a range of contexts including home, school, church, at the park, at the beach and with candles. A number of children noted the significance of praying in either the privacy of their bedroom or outdoors. There were also several Muslim children who identified praying at the mosque and at home with their families. For many children, it was clear that prayer was an important part of their everyday life which was facilitated by school but which extended far beyond that into individual rituals and practices.

From this research, for primary school children the practice of prayer seems to be the practice which is most consistent across the different spheres of home, church and school and connects the three in unexpected and surprising ways. However, references to church were very limited when it came to children exploring their prayer lives. This may have been because the question they were asked was very open and didn't specifically ask about church. However, while children had structured prayer time within their school contexts and had developed their own rhythms and practices at home (including outdoor activities), church was referenced in much smaller ways. This isn't necessarily a bad thing, but when families often face criticism from church leaders for not taking a more active role in faith development (as explored in Chapter 6) it's interesting to note that children's prayer lives are flourishing. This reality should challenge all those involved in church ministry. I wonder what it might mean for churches to learn from schools and households about prayer? How can children take the lead in praying in our church congregations? What might we learn from their preferences for praying outdoors or in the quiet of their bedrooms? How might any of these insights disrupt or challenge the ways we encourage children and teenagers to pray within churches?

There was a noticeable shift in the conversation around prayer when it came to secondary school pupils. The overwhelming response was that prayer was something they either don't do at all or something they used to do; and a number of pupils chose not to respond to this question at all. This may have been due to the focus group context the discussions were held in as young people will only be willing to share what they feel comfortable with among their peers. Alongside this large majority, there was a small minority of pupils who had a clearly expressed Christian faith and other children who acknowledged that, while they don't pray currently, they would know what to do if they needed to. This included a Year 8 pupil who commented: 'I'm not that religious but if I've got something going on that I'm stressed about I just pray.' As outlined in other chapters, the significance of family relationships was emphasized again, with several young people identifying prayer happening within their broader family context and one Year 11 pupil reflecting 'I don't [pray], but if I did want to I'd go round me grandma's house.' School provided a substantial scaffold for prayer within secondary schools, with pupils in all year groups referencing daily prayer and worship within their school contexts. However, it was clear that pupils were fully aware this was something that, while compulsory, they had the freedom to choose how they engaged with it.

It is striking to reflect on the substantial difference in numbers between the 13 per cent of primary-school-aged children who weren't praying and over 35 per cent (of those who chose to respond to the question) of secondary school pupils. This secondary school figure is likely to be even higher when other variations in the data are considered, but the clear trend is that while prayer is something which is engaged with extensively across the primary school year groups in a range of contexts, by secondary school this has drastically reduced. This could be related to how willing secondary school pupils are to discuss their inner spiritual lives, although they were confident in giving responses and contributions to other discussion questions. It also raises a big question about how schools and churches in particular can support the transition from primary to secondary school and how teenagers are able to explore, develop and deepen their prayer lives.

There is another big, related question, which is particularly for churches, church leaders and youth ministry leaders, about how to support faith and spirituality in secondary schools. When the secondary school pupils were asked about which adults in their lives helped them to think about God and faith, only two young people across both secondary schools referenced a church leader! This may well be due to the local context and the specific relationships the schools had with local church leaders, however, it was a stark reality. For these young people, teachers and family members were those who had the biggest influence, particularly RE teachers and grandparents. Church leaders had very little influence on their faith and spiritual landscape. This relates back to the significance of community and family relationships we explored throughout this book, but it also offers a challenge for churches and church leaders to reflect on where they can build relationships, support and engage with young people within secondary schools. As will be made clear in the final section of this chapter, children and young people are asking big questions and they don't always have the space or confidence to explore them.

## Big questions

Teenagers often get a bad reputation, particularly when it comes to talking to adults. We can assume that they aren't interested in talking about faith or the big things in life. But this research showed again and again that teenagers particularly are thinking about enormous questions and they're often wondering and reflecting in deep and profound ways. We asked the secondary school pupils what kind of questions they were asking about being a Christian or matters of faith in general. The most overwhelming responses were: 'Is it real?', 'Does God actually exist?' and could they believe any of it? These were young people who were searching and wondering and questioning and what they needed was a space to ask these questions out loud, not necessarily to receive any answers immediately, but just to speak and discuss and ponder. I was so powerfully struck by some of the questions that I have included them here. This list isn't exhaustive, but it is both inspiring and challenging and gives a small and privileged insight into the lives of these young people:

- How can God write a book that's on earth even though people weren't alive when he made the world? How can someone

## SCHOOL COMMUNITIES

write about something when they weren't there? Is God real or do people just have voices in their head?
- The one question that never leaves my mind entirely is why do bad things happen to good people?
- Why does God make the decisions that he does? Like why does war happen and why do people die and why can't people just ... I don't know ... not block you on Snapchat?
- If God is all-knowing and all-loving why does suffering exist?
- Is death the end? Is there another reality?
- I would like to know if there is life on other planets.
- Why are we here?
- If we grow up in the same place, why are people so different? Why do some go on to become criminals?
- If scientific theories are true, is it God testing us whether we believe in him?
- Does God know every single thing that will happen? We have free will but is this really my choice?
- Is God man or girl?
- Everyone claims that God is benevolent and all-knowing and that, but then lets a bunch of bad things happen to people.
- Why do people change to Christianity in mid-life because you should have to stay loyal not change halfway through.
- One thing where you think if God says to be kind to everybody why would he also not include gay people in that?
- How did Jesus come back to life?

A number of these amazing questions were accompanied by comments that the young people did not have a space to ask or discuss these questions. There wasn't space in their timetables for these kinds of conversations and many of them weren't sure which adult they could speak to about this. It strikes me that the church could play a significant role in creating space for these kinds of conversations; for enabling young people to wonder and question, for providing a theological structure for exploring answers and some hope in the darkness and uncertainty. I wonder if there are ways in which both school and church leaders could work together to enable a space in which conversations like this could happen more readily? Sometimes teenagers need someone outside their usual frame of reference to have these conversations with and there is a huge opportunity here for relationships to be built and for these questions to be heard.

## Conclusion

Within this chapter, we've heard the voices of children and young people exploring God, faith, the Bible, prayer and big questions. The conversations we had were rich, beautiful, diverse and challenging! I've shared just a small sample here but I hope that it offers food for thought, reflection and that the questions raised might inspire, encourage and challenge all those involved with ministry in schools, households and churches – as well as the many spaces in between.

### *Notes*

1 With thanks to Claire Lewis and Ana Moskvina who acted as research assistants on this project. Thank you also to the headteachers, staff and students who shared so openly and honestly with us. We have kept the identities of the school contexts and students confidential and all data has been fully anonymized. Full ethical approval was granted for this project by Durham University.

# 8

# Navigating Change: A Theological and Practical Model of Change for Growth

## EMMA L. PARKER

The word 'change' can cause an automatic reaction in each of us. Some of us might be filled with adrenaline-fuelled excitement at the thought of change bringing fresh challenge and opportunities. Others might be filled with dread and reach for the handbrake. Many factors can shape our reaction to change: our previous experience of it, how we have observed others reacting to it, our age, personality and character, to name a few. We might instantly think of the glorious chance for something to be transformed for the better, or of the terrible risk for something to dwindle or even be lost for ever. Whether our initial reaction to change is positive or negative, change can often be demanding in many ways.

Change often requires us to inhabit a new set of rules or guidelines, or develop a new mindset. As such it needs more of our focus and concentration, which can be physically, emotionally and mentally exhausting. Change might require us to adopt different roles: we might need to become the leader or learn how to follow another leader. We might need to operate outside our comfort zone and learn new skills, or we might finally get a chance to use some skills that never normally see the light of day. Change might be a place where we thrive, or a place where we just about survive. It might be the arena where we find a degree of power, or where we become suddenly powerless and vulnerable. It might be the place of celebrating life, or of grieving loss.

Our reaction to change can largely depend on the speed and the type of change. There are different degrees of change, from slight alterations to a complete transformation. These types of changes still involve a fair degree of consistency, where the object of the change remains the same at heart, but it is reshaped, edited and amended. A visit to the groomers means my dog will return home as a dog but looking and smelling much better! Practising an instrument or a language every day will result in the improvement of a skill. Sometimes a goal or aim remains the same, but how we reach that goal changes. A long journey might involve changing trains several times but they all serve the same purpose in helping the passenger travel from one place to another. Dinner might suddenly change from jollof rice to chicken and chips when you realize you have run out of rice, but the goal of eating has not changed. Change can be about reaching a goal, perfecting something, making something more beautiful or helpful. However, it can also be the opposite where it involves deterioration, as the hymn 'Abide with me' says: 'Change and decay in all around I see'.[1]

Regardless of how we might personally react to change, it has become apparent throughout this book that in thinking theologically and practically about ministry with children and young people, our churches need to embrace change to some degree. Perhaps we have realized that the way our own church views children needs to change from them being gifts of the future church to blessings in the present one. Perhaps there needs to be a shift in attitude and perspective towards the importance of children in the church and in the kingdom. We might be persuaded that our church needs to change from being multigenerational to intergenerational for the growth of the faith of our children and young people, *and* for the whole body. In other words, the default shifts from nurturing faith and discipleship in age-based groups to all-age groups. Our thoughts might be focused on how we can worship, learn and minister as one body, all ages together, all ages offering their gifts, and all ages discerning their calling from God. We might be considering how we can support our different households and encourage the parents, carers and grandparents in enabling faith to grow in their family. Perhaps we are wondering how to listen to the voices of children in our churches and schools. The ways in which our churches need to change could range from needing small adjustments to radical transformation either in the culture or the practice (or both). To make what might seem a small surface change might require a deeper, more substantial change in how the congregation understands the place of children and young people – and then we find ourselves in the arena of the ethos, theology and culture.

Even if our church has children and young people present, we still need to be aware of how we must develop this ministry first to keep on serving our children and young people in the best way we can offer, and second because the world is constantly changing. Deborah Rowland writes: 'Change has ceased to be about one-off set piece events and has morphed into an ongoing endemic phenomenon.'[2] The ever-changing world (with increasing interaction between the local and the global) can bring with it new questions, new challenges, new opportunities, new threats and new ideas to Christ's body – and specifically to how we can grow in faith together, and grow in our relationships across the generations. Alternatively, if our church currently has no or very few children and young people, this signals that there is a significant, but not impossible, journey of change in which to participate.

In this chapter, we will therefore explore some models of change before looking at what it might mean to have a theology of change – how we see and understand change within Scripture and within the call to follow Christ as pilgrim people. From this I propose a new model of change, which arises from theology and practice, and which takes account of the urgency and complexity of change our churches face in growing together in faith, and in growing in faith together.

## Tools and models in navigating change

As we think of children, churches and change, we first need to spend time praying, thinking of our goal and discerning the vision. After this, we need to explore the strategy for reaching the vision. Unless vision has a strategy, it is simply an idea among many that will never make a difference. This section does not explore how churches can discern the vision but rather offers some tools and models that have been created to help implement the cultural or practical change that is needed to reach the vision. It will therefore help in considering strategy, but the focus will be on navigating change as part of the strategy.

There are many different models of how to lead change. Some offer a chronological order of steps and others offer more of a jigsaw piece approach where each piece is important, but not the order in which they are placed in the picture. Cory Siebel, for example, in writing about changing from a multigenerational to an intergenerational church, uses the framework based on Everett Rogers's model which has five chronological stages.[3] The first is about the importance of creating an awareness of the problem or issues facing the church, which then leads to the second stage of helping members develop a deeper understanding of these issues. Once this has been achieved, the congregation can move to the third phase of evaluating their church (both its culture and practice) through the lens of this new understanding and begin to make decisions about change. The fourth stage is the time for action and experimentation. Siebel writes: 'As people experiment with what they have been learning, true cultural change can become embedded in the life of the congregation.'[4] The final stage is commitment, where the church continues to put into action their understanding of, and insights into being, an intergenerational church. This provides a helpful and neat tool for churches to use in managing change. However, it is based on the view that the whole congregation can come to one mind and move as one. While this is optimal, it is probably unrealistic in most congregations.

A very different model is offered by Deborah Rowland, which acknowledges the complexity of change and the importance of the role of the leader.[5] She argues that leaders of change need eight skills, four of which are about being 'still' in the midst of leading change and focusing on 'qualities of *being*', and the other four are about 'moving' and are 'qualities of *doing*'.[6] The four 'still' skills include leaders firstly being able to notice what they are experiencing themselves, including their 'inner thoughts, feelings, sensations and impulses', and then secondly being able to 'slow down the period between experience and reaction'.[7] This helps leaders not to respond impulsively and from habit, but to do so intentionally. The next two 'still' skills widen the focus to the organization, where the leader thirdly 'tunes into the system' to gain a deeper understanding of reality and therefore of what needs to be changed, while also demonstrating the fourth skill of being able to observe all the experiences in the organization, particularly the 'difficulty and disturbance'.[8] The four 'moving' skills include the leader's ability to: (i) attract others towards the need for change, (ii) name and confront the challenges and handbrakes, and (iii) channel anxiety into positive and productive energy.[9] Finally, leaders need to be able to combine these three skills to create a transforming and safe space where the organization moves further towards its purpose and members can 'boldly experiment with a new mindset and a new voice'.[10] This model provides a rich and helpful tool that focuses on leadership skills rather than a step-by-step approach and pays attention to the difficulties that surface in change. Some of these skills, however, are in themselves complex and can take years of experience and good mentoring to develop.

As with all models, we need to look at models of change like a toolbox and discern which tools we need for our particular job in our particular context. Models are helpful up to a point and it is important we equip ourselves by exploring these and potentially adding new tools to our own contextually shaped toolbox.[11] However, it is also important to consider the theology underpinning change and see how this shapes our own approach to change. In the next section I present a new model that takes account of the complexity of change within our churches, and which arises from theology and practice.

# A theology of change for a practical model of growth: listening, weaving, climbing, praying

It is important to ask if we have a theology of change. In other words, how do we understand and articulate the story of change in Scripture, in relating to God, and in having faith? The New Testament picture of discipleship is undeniably about change and transformation. The very act of being baptized means we have been buried with Christ so that we 'might walk in newness of life' (Rom. 6.4). Paul urges his readers to 'be transformed by the renewing of your minds' (Rom. 12.2); and those who are 'in Christ' are part of God making all things new (2 Cor. 5.17). The hope is that we are being transformed into the likeness of Christ, 'from one degree of glory to another' (2 Cor. 3.18) and so we sing: 'Changed from glory into glory, till in heav'n we take our place, till we cast our crowns before thee, lost in wonder, love and praise.'[12] In addition to this expectation for spiritual change in the followers of Christ, there are also stories that describe events of change throughout Scripture. In these stories we find repeated patterns of how God helps his people to navigate change: listening, weaving, climbing and praying. We will now turn to explore these patterns and discover how they can help our churches to minister with the younger generation.

## 1 – Listening

Throughout the Old Testament, God engages his people in conversation, especially at key moments of change. He invites them to share their experiences, questions and doubts, and involves them in debate and reasoning.[13] Thus, when Moses is first called by God, and is therefore standing on the precipice of monumental change for him personally, and for the Israelites as a whole, God listens to his objections, his fears and his questions (Ex. 3.11, 13, 4.1, 10, 13). He responds to each in turn by giving practical signs or assurances of help (4.2–9, 11–12, 14–16) and by telling Moses more of the bigger plan for deliverance (3.14–22). When

Elijah is fearing for his life after he carries out his prophetic call to challenge and change King Ahab's idolatry and worship of Baal, he flees into the wilderness and eventually finds himself hiding in a cave (1 Kings 19.1–9). God asks twice: 'What are you doing here, Elijah?' (19.9, 13). Each time God allows Elijah to tell his story and describe his fear, before God answers and reveals more of himself and of his plan (19.11–13, 15–18). When God saw the repentance of Nineveh and 'changed his mind' about punishing them (Jonah 3.10), Jonah became angry about God's unchanging merciful and loving nature (4.1–2). God then asks him a question and uses a practical illustration to draw Jonah into a conversation in which he reveals his concern for the salvation of a whole nation (Jonah 4.4–11). God repeatedly invites storytelling. He listens and then responds by weaving this story into his own metanarrative of salvation.

Jesus continues this in the New Testament where he listens to people's stories (particularly ones of longing for change) and then links these with his story of redemption. When Jesus met the man who had been ill for 38 years, lying by the pool 'Bethesda', he asked him a question (John 5.6), listened to his story (v. 7), and then responded with a command, 'Stand up, take your mat and walk' (v. 8). The command invited the man to step into Jesus' own story of healing. In the story of the healing of the Canaanite woman's daughter (Matt. 15.21–28), it is the woman who initiates the conversation with Jesus (v. 22). Although at first Jesus does not answer (v. 23), a conversation ensues (vv. 24–28) in which the mother determinedly challenges Jesus to change her story (into one of healing) *and* his story (to be present for those outside the house of Israel). When Mary and Martha were grieving the death of their brother Lazarus, Jesus listened to them each saying that his earlier presence could have stopped this unwanted change and prevented this tragedy (John 11.21, 32). He responded by telling them more about his own identity ('I am the resurrection and the life', v. 25) and then demonstrated this by raising Lazarus from death (vv. 43–44). He put his words into action and thus wove his story of resurrection into their story of loss and grief. As such, we uncover a pattern of divine listening and weaving: listening to people's stories and experiences particularly in times of change, and then weaving these into the overarching story of redemption.

Brueggemann offers an interesting observation that, when combined with the observation above, brings more insight into this listening-weaving pattern. He argues that the prophetic teaching of Jesus 'presumed a contrast between that to which we cling and a future for which we yearn', and that the ministry of Jesus 'happens in the space between the clinging and the yearning'.[14] The divine act of listening begins by stepping into wherever the story is located: either in the space of clinging or of yearning. Yet the divine act of weaving occurs in the middle space between the clinging and yearning, the location of redemption and salvation history. Divine listening encounters the stories of clinging and yearning, and divine weaving draws these stories into the middle space, the space of Jesus' ministry.

Hence, I propose that one of the most important steps in either leading or helping to steer change in our churches, is participating in this divine act of listening to the previous and present stories of change in the church and wider community. This will not only help the listener to 'acknowledge the whole' in hearing the fears and the hopes but also identify the locations of these stories.[15] On the one hand, this will reveal the stories of longing where people see the famine and hope for a feast. On the other hand, it will reveal the things to which people cling tightly – not meaning those aspects of faith which anchor our identity in Christ, but rather the way in which we can take aspects of our practice or of life in general, idolize them, cling to them, and in so doing, potentially become divisive and exclusive.

In thinking about ministry with children and teenagers and how our churches need to change, it is important to listen and locate the places of clinging and yearning. Do the places of clinging or longing have only one generation present, and are they different in each place? Where are the voices of children to be found? When these stories are told are there any repeated phrases (e.g. 'I wish we could … ', or, 'We used to … ')? For example, many years ago I worked as the parish priest in a former coal mining community that could still vividly remember the strikes, the clashes with police, and the division in the community between those who joined the picket line in striking and those who kept on working. The phrase used to describe the impact of the closure of the mine was that it 'ripped the heart out' of the community. As such, in 2015, a nine-foot steel statue was erected in a community park which depicted a miner with his heart ripped out.[16] This was almost 30 years after the pit was closed in this particular town, but nevertheless, the community still grieved the closure of the pit and the resulting change from being a place with purpose and identity to a place that had lost its heart. The story of change was one of decay in which some people felt they had fought and lost, made enemies of friends, and lost communal identity and pride.

Here I discovered the clinging to wounds, to grief, to memories of a tight-knit community which valued close friendships and took pride in its achievements and purpose. Some of the clinging was so strong however that it meant the idea of hope was about returning to the days when the pit wheel turned, rather than how to reimagine new ways of church and community for the present, bringing young and old together and having a vision that helped us to journey onward. I realized that some forms of clinging have the capacity to close off spirit-led imagination, and fear of change can be about fear of failure and of loss. There was, however, also yearning. Many people were desperate for positive change, to explore new ideas, to make new stories, to take risks and seek to be inclusive; and these people had been waiting a long time.

However, the aim of listening to these stories of change and locating the places of clinging and longing, is to discern how to weave them into the middle place, into the metanarrative of salvation. For, after listening, comes weaving.

## 2 – *Weaving*

We have already seen how, in moments of change, the divine act of listening leads to a weaving of the fears, hopes, objections and questions of the storyteller into God's story of redemption. What begins with God's act of listening (to his people's story), ends with his people listening to God's story – which then becomes their story as they find themselves woven into the middle space of Jesus' ministry. Sometimes this weaving happens simply by God teaching more about himself and his plan of salvation. For example, in the Beatitudes (Matt. 5.2–12; Luke 6.20–23), Jesus teaches us that 'the options presented to us by the world are not all that there is. There remains a better way and that better way is the kingdom of God.'[17] At other times the weaving involves signs and acts to provide people with the courage or the faith to listen in turn to his story. These signs could be anything from changing Moses' staff into a snake and back again (Ex. 4.1–5), to Jesus helping Simon, James and John with a miraculous catch of fish and inviting them into a new story of fishing for people (Luke 5.1–11). They are signs of God's glory, signs of a new way, signs of new life. The signs function as threads, drawing us closer and closer into the middle space where we find a better way, a better story.

Thus, in navigating change in our churches, we need to discern how to weave the threads of teaching and of signs into the stories we have heard, to enable a movement of people into the middle space, and a transformation from the ways of the world into the better way of the kingdom. For example, after listening to the stories of change in the parish above, I realized the importance of not radically changing everything thereby adding to the wound of grief. I therefore set about making small additions which were intentionally all age, and which became the threads of change. We started a lunchtime group of crafts and food during the school holidays (aptly called 'Messy Lunch') and a gospel choir that gathered people from outside and inside different churches and communities. We started different projects with the schools that involved creating prayer galleries in the church or a children's choir that sang with a local opera singer. We started a new contemporary evening service, a weekly prayer walk and a shop in the church for pre-loved baby clothes.

Gradually, people of all ages started to move from the places of clinging and yearning into the middle space. Some found their faith transformed and some found faith for the first time. New stories of change were created, and these were stories of wonder and joy. We began to grow a church community that cared for each other, was excited by its purpose and which delighted in seeing how God was doing new things. I began to see that those things to which people were clinging from their memories (identity, belonging, purpose, community) were the things people were yearning for in the present. Now, however, they were being made a reality in this new, hope-filled, faith community, in the space between the clinging and the yearning, where there is a better way, where Jesus stands ministering. The act of listening to people's stories enabled an act of weaving whereby together we began to seriously listen to God's story of hope for us all.

One day, one of the parents who had joined church in this middle space came to tell me that her daughter was thinking about going to college after leaving school. She would be the first one in her family to stay in education after the age of 16. I joined in with her joy and asked what her daughter would like to do at college. 'Well', she said, 'she's thinking about childcare, but I told her she could be a vicar! She's doing a GCSE in Religious Studies and she likes drinking tea and talking to people so she could do it if she wanted, couldn't she?!' That this mum could imagine her daughter being a vicar and was proud of this dream spoke powerfully of the weaving process. For this was happening in an area where confidence and self-esteem were low, where few children had any aspirations, where imagination did not pay the bills and where, up until recently, church was not a place for children and young people. Delight surged through my spirit as I knew in that moment we were creating a new narrative of change, filled with grace and hope, which pictured a better way, and where we really saw Jesus at work.

In your own churches, what new threads could you use to

weave the local stories you have heard into the cosmic story of grace? What threads of teaching and of signs might enable people to leave their places of clinging and yearning, and be drawn into the middle space and find Jesus? Rowan Williams writes: 'A healthy church is one in which we seek to stay connected with God by seeking to connect others with God.'[18] How might our weaving create new, and tighten existing connections with God, thereby helping the church to grow together in faith, and grow in faith together?

## 3 – Climbing

As we read through different narratives of change in Scripture, alongside God's act of listening and weaving, we also find God inviting those involved in change to climb a mountain. It is when Moses came to Mount Horeb that 'the angel of the LORD appeared to him in a flame of fire out of a bush' (Ex. 3.1–2), and from which God called Moses to help with the freeing of the Israelites from captivity in Egypt. After the exodus, God called Moses to join him on Mount Sinai where he promised to give him tablets of stone with the 'law and the commandment' (Ex. 24.12–18). Just before Moses dies, and before the Israelites cross the Jordan into the promised land, the Lord again called Moses to go up another mountain (Mount Nebo) to show him the extent of this land, since he himself would not enter it (Deut. 32.48–49, 34.1–5).

In the New Testament, Jesus often went up a mountain at significant transitions in his ministry. Jesus' transfiguration happens after he invites some of the Disciples up a mountain with him to pray, and during this remarkable scene of revelation, Moses and Elijah are also seen talking with Jesus (Luke 9.28–36; Matt. 17.1–8). It is when they had reached the Mount of Olives that Jesus instructed the Disciples to find a donkey and a colt to prepare for his entry into Jerusalem, the final journey before his betrayal, arrest and crucifixion (Matt. 21.1; Mark 11.1). From this mountain Jesus prayed in anguish, was strengthened by an angel, betrayed with a kiss, and arrested amid swords (Luke 22.39–53). After Jesus' resurrection, the 'eleven disciples went to Galilee, to the mountain to which Jesus had directed them' (Matt. 28.16). From this mountain Jesus appears to them, commissions them to 'make disciples of all nations' and reminds them of his abiding presence (vv. 18–20).

Clearly, mountains are places associated with God's activity and revelation at key turning points in salvation history. However, climbing a mountain also enables a sense of perspective. Climbing to a height enabled Moses to see the bigger picture of the journey he had taken, where his will end, and where it will continue for Joshua. Climbing the mountain surely inspired and enabled the Disciples at their commissioning to look across and imagine all the nations of the world receiving the teaching of the good news of Christ. Likewise, when we ascend the mountain, we have a better sense of perspective of the journey we have already taken and the one still to come. When I first moved to Durham city I found it puzzling how my daily walk into the town centre involved crossing the same river several times. It wasn't until I ascended the 325 steps in the cathedral tower that I could then appreciate the meandering nature of the River Wear. Being able to see the bigger picture brought insight and understanding. Thus, surely the Disciples, on seeing Jesus' transfiguration at the top of the mountain, had a renewed sense of understanding of how to follow Jesus at the bottom of the mountain.

There is something sacred and significant about climbing higher especially in a time of change or transition, in gaining a bigger sense of reality and of eternity, seeing a different and magnificent dimension in God's picture that simply cannot be seen or appreciated from below. As such, in thinking of our own context and journey of change, where might God be calling us to climb the mountain to gain a greater understanding of his own nature, or a better perspective of the journey he is guiding us on? When we are at the bottom of the mountain and we are becoming saturated with listening, our arms are getting tired of weaving, and we have lost track of where the middle space is, we need to step out and step up – we need to climb to get a greater perspective.

The climbing creates a sacred pause in the chaos and offers relief from being submerged in detail. The climbing creates a point of encouragement for the church, a place of celebration to recognize the journey so far. The metaphorical mountain could be a church day away at a retreat centre, or a prayer day in another church hall. It could be anything: just as long as there is space to see, reflect, pause and worship in wonder. And this leads us to our final pattern for change: prayer.

## 4 – *Praying*

When we return once more to the points of change in Scripture, we see that prayer is a pattern that runs through these stories. There are songs of praise celebrating key transition points or pointing to miraculous transformation to come. Hannah prays a song of praise after leaving her son Samuel at the temple (1 Samuel 2.1–10), and Deborah and Barak sing of God's power after they defeated King Jabin of Canaan and his commander, Sisera (Judges 5). In Luke 1.46–55 we hear Mary pray a song of fearless hope while Zechariah praises God (1.64) and announces a prophecy (vv. 67–79). There are also prayers of lament, praying and hoping for God's justice and deliverance: for example, Jonah from inside the whale (Jonah 2), David's songs of lament throughout the psalms (e.g. 57, 59, 61) and Jesus' own prayer from the Garden of Gethsemane (Matt. 26.36–46; Mark 14.32–42; Luke 22.39–46). Prayer is not only a pattern of navigating change but also a way of life for God's people.

Prayer is essential. David Adam writes: 'Mission has often failed because people have sought to talk about God when they have not yet talked enough to him.'[19] We could apply this to everything we do in church. Every aspect of mission and ministry, including change, can fail because we do not spend enough time intentionally praying to God. We can also fall into the erroneous practice of using prayer as a warm-up exercise before the 'real' ministry. Prayer, however, is not just the beginning of change, of ministry, or of mission, but it is the way in which we do all these things. Prayer is how we change, how we serve and how we minister. Prayer is how we participate in the divine acts of listening and weaving, and it is how we climb the mountain and pause. Margaret Silf writes:

> If there is no connection between the prayer we express with our mouths, and even in our hearts, and the place where we put our time, our energy, our resources and our passion, then nothing is going to change, however assiduously we pray that it should.[20]

Silf urges disciples to connect their prayers to their actions. Conversely, in navigating change, we must ensure that we connect our actions of change to our prayers. Thus, as we lead or help to navigate change in our churches, we must prioritize prayer and pray continually.

After the first six months in one of my parishes, I felt God telling me to pause before setting up a whole new range of groups and services. I felt some pressure to start new things or restart old things, which came from both the place of clinging and of yearning. I felt God saying, 'Just pray.' It dawned on me that spiritual revival, change and transformation will never happen unless we have a prayer revival. When we are seeking change in our churches, we need to be passionate and committed to praying at every step, otherwise we may end up creating a kingdom that is more about ourselves than about Christ, and connect others' stories to our own rather than to God's. As such, we started a 'prayer revival meeting' where we gathered once a month to share lunch, deepen our understanding of prayer, and then pray together.

Change must always begin with and be fuelled by prayer. There needs to be a culture of prayer, where people believe in prayer because they believe in God's care, in God's faithfulness, and in God's desire for all people of all ages and all nations to connect to his story of salvation. The first step in helping a church to grow faith in all ages, and to grow together in faith, might actually be to help it grow in prayer.

# Conclusion

If we are serious about growth and serious about the presence, worship and ministry of our children and young people in our churches, then our churches need to change. We can borrow tools from some excellent models of change and seek to develop our skills as leaders of change, but first and foremost we need to consider our theology of change. Scripture is itself a metanarrative of change, revealing how God journeys with his people to help them connect more and more to his kingdom of grace and his story of redemption. In enabling our churches to change, we need to begin by participating in God's act of listening and locate the stories in the places of clinging or longing. We then need to discern how to weave these stories into the story of redemption found in the middle space. Climbing the mountain (whether metaphorical or physical) will enable us and our churches to gain a better perspective of the journey behind and ahead, and a greater understanding of God. And finally, we do all these things in, and through prayer. Growing in prayer will be the catalyst for growing in faith together, and growing together in faith.

## Notes

1 From verse 2 of the hymn, 'Abide with me' by Henry Francis Lyte.

2 D. Rowland, 2017, *Still Moving: How to Lead Mindful Change*, Chichester: Wiley Blackwell, p. 215.

3 E. M. Rogers, 2003, *Diffusion of Innovations*, fifth edition, New York: Free Press. Quoted in C. Siebel, 2018, 'From *multi*generational to *inter*generational', in H. C. Allen (ed.), *InterGenerate: Transforming Churches through Intergenerational Ministry*, Abilene, TX: Abilene Christian University Press, pp. 87–98.

4 Siebel, 'From *multi*generational to *inter*generational', p. 94.

5 This model arises from Rowland's experience and research of leading change in large national and international companies and organizations, but the skills she suggests are ones that are important in leading change within churches.

6 Rowland, *Still Moving*, p. 218.

7 Rowland, *Still Moving*, p. 218.

8 Rowland, *Still Moving*, p. 220.

9 Rowland, *Still Moving*, pp. 220–1.

10 D. Rowland and M. Higgs, 2008, *Sustaining Change: Leadership That Works*, San Francisco, CA: Jossey-Bass, p. 273.

11 In Chapter 5 of her book, Margaret Pritchard Houston refers to a few different models of change and then specifically suggests how these can be used as tools in managing change in our churches. M. P. Houston, 2020, *Beyond the Children's Corner: Creating a Culture of Welcome for All Ages*, London: Church House Publishing.

12 From verse 4 of the hymn, 'Love Divine' by Charles Wesley.

13 In Isaiah God says, 'Come now, let us argue it out' (1.18), or 'let us reason' (KJV).

14 W. Brueggemann, 2018, *The Prophetic Imagination: 40th Anniversary Edition*, Minneapolis, MN: Fortress Press, p. 111.

15 Rowland, *Still Moving*, p. 220. This is also about 'tuning into the system' where a deeper way of seeing reality is uncovered, which can then lead to a 'powerful diagnosis of what needs changing' (p. 220).

16 The statue is called 'Marra' and was made by Ray Lonsdale and is erected in Horden Welfare Park.

17 E. McCaulley, 2020, *Reading While Black: African American Biblical Interpretation as an Exercise in Hope*, Downers Grove, IL: InterVarsity Press, p. 66.

18 R. Williams, 2003, *Silence and Honey Cakes: The Wisdom of the Desert*, Oxford: Lion Books, p. 34.

19 D. Adams, 2006, *Aidan, Bede, Cuthbert: Three Inspirational Saints*, London: SPCK, p. 33.

20 M. Silf, 2004, *Companions of Christ: Ignatian Spirituality for Everyday Living*, Norwich: Canterbury Press, p. 98.

# Concluding Thoughts

This book began with the question, 'Why?' It ends with another question, 'Why not?' When we understand how important children and teenagers are to God and to the community of faith, and when we consider the practical ways for building intergenerational faith communities, why would we not invest in ministry with children and teenagers? There will always be challenges and hurdles when creating or developing an intergenerational faith community, but these can be overcome when our theology drives our passion and belief in the importance of children and teenagers. Throughout this book we have consistently seen, through biblical evidence and contemporary research, that children and teenagers play a significant role in the life of the body of Christ, and that intergenerational relationships rooted in Christ are the catalyst for growth and transformation.

Chapter 1 uncovered the special relationship that God has with children. We have been challenged to ensure that we see the image of God in children and teenagers and to think about how Jesus' teaching about children and the kingdom shapes not only our own discipleship but also the vision and culture of the whole church. There is a sacred connection between the presence of children and the presence of Christ and it is vital that our churches participate in this sacred welcome.

Chapter 2 encouraged us to look beyond the purely knowledge-based aspects of faith development models to a forest-based image of faith development rooted in Jesus Christ. Faith development is an intergenerational, communal act of growing together, rather than something that adults aim to instil in children or teenagers. There is a mutuality here founded in trusting relation-

## CONCLUDING THOUGHTS

ships, imagination, play, questions and storytelling which are all key features of an intergenerational community that grows in faith together throughout the seasons of life.

Further exploration through the Old Testament and New Testament in Chapter 3 showed the expectation that children should be included in hearing God's Word, witnessing his actions and responding in worship within the wider faith community. Hence, not only were children shaped by the faith story they received, they also contributed to the ongoing development of this story as they discerned God's ways and responded with trust. Through the different stories of children like Moses, David, the enslaved girl and the boy with the lunch, we saw the need for adults to encourage children's gifts and offerings, to humbly receive ministry from them, and to receive the theological perspectives they bring to how we can navigate challenges and opportunities. This exploration led us to conclude that intergenerational faith communities are important in God's own vision for his people.

Chapter 4 therefore examined the nature and character of intergenerational churches today, where it was proposed that different generations bring different gifts in forming the community's identity and purpose. These different generations enable the whole community to join memory with hope, and to discern how to live faithfully within their wider communities and as powerful witnesses of God's work of reconciliation. We looked at the relationship between belief and belonging, and offered different practical ways for intergenerational learning to take place so that faith can grow as relationships deepen.

The importance of intergenerational churches was continued in Chapter 5, with a focus on worship, ministry and vocation. We argued that intergenerational worship seeks to bring all ages together in encountering God and in being transformed as a whole body by God. It seeks to enable all ages to lead and participate in worship in a way that can edify all members of the body. Furthermore, intergenerational worship can provide opportunities to help children and teenagers not only find purpose by serving in different ways, but also by helping them to discern how God is calling them to use their particular gifts and skills for the mission and ministry of the church. Intergenerational faith communities have a heightened anticipation of how God will act through all ages and call all ages to be part of his transformation, and an increased wonder in perceiving God doing a new thing through the youngest child and the oldest adult.

Chapter 6 surveyed the reality and complexity of twenty-first-century family life before drawing on biblical and theological resources to develop a theology of household faith. A challenge was offered to church leaders to change their approach to supporting family faith at home through attentive listening and building deeper relationships to ensure they understand the particular needs of the families they serve.

Chapter 7 amplified the voices of over 400 children and teenagers through school-based empirical research. School pupils from the ages of 4 to 16 from across the north-east of England responded to questions of faith, prayer and engagement with the Bible, and they in turn shared their reflections on some of their own key questions about faith and life. This research highlighted the significant role of school vision and values on the shape of children's faith and the important role of adults as conversation partners in faith and theology. It also revealed a substantial shift in approaches and engagement with prayer between primary school and secondary school, alongside a gap in church contributions within secondary school contexts. Overall, it emphasized the unique faith landscape of each child and the importance of listening and responding to the voices of children and teenagers as we seek to grow in faith together.

Finally, in Chapter 8 we named the need for our churches to either embark on a fresh journey of change to become places where all ages can grow together in faith, or to keep on developing as intergenerational faith communities. As such, after looking at some models of change, we explored a theological understanding of change: how change and transformation are naturally part of being 'in Christ', and part of being connected to God's story of redemption for all nations. A new theological and practical model was proposed which seeks to mirror how God helps his people to navigate change throughout Scripture.

## CONCLUDING THOUGHTS

This involves: (i) listening to people's experiences and stories and locating these in the places of clinging or longing; (ii) weaving these stories into the metanarrative of salvation, by helping people to step into the place where Christ's redemptive work is found; (iii) climbing above the detail and chaos to find a fresh perspective or insight into God's presence and guidance; and (iv) praying throughout all these steps so that prayer becomes the fuel needed in navigating change. Prayer recognizes our need for God to be the ultimate leader of our change and transformation.

Growing together in faith is about growing deeper into the vision God has for his people, where young and old flourish in faith and use their gifts to grow his kingdom here on earth. As all ages grow together in richer, more meaningful relationships across the generations, the faith of all ages grows as the whole body encounters the transforming presence of God. And thus, in answering the question 'Why?', we simply point to Christ, who points to the child, who then points back to us and asks, 'Why not?'

# Index of Biblical References

## Old Testament

*Genesis*
| | |
|---|---|
| 1.26, 28 | 7 |
| 1.1—2.4 | 7 |
| 5.1b–2 | 7 |
| 9.6 | 7 |
| 37—50 | 64 |

*Exodus*
| | |
|---|---|
| 2.1–10 | 48, 71 |
| 3.1–2 | 128 |
| 3.3–4 | 64 |
| 3.11 | 122 |
| 3.13 | 122 |
| 3.14–22 | 122 |
| 4.1–5 | 126 |
| 4.1–16 | 122 |
| 12.26–27 | 43 |
| 24.12–18 | 128 |

*Deuteronomy*
| | |
|---|---|
| 6 | 92 |
| 6.4–9 | 43 |
| 11.18–21 | 92 |
| 29 | 92 |
| 29.10–11 | 43 |
| 31.10–13 | 92 |
| 31.12–13 | 43 |
| 32.48–49 | 128 |
| 34.1–5 | 128 |

*Joshua*
| | |
|---|---|
| 8.34–35 | 43 |

*Judges*
| | |
|---|---|
| 5 | 130 |

*1 Samuel*
| | |
|---|---|
| 1.9–11 | 45 |
| 1.19–28 | 45 |
| 2.1–10 | 130 |
| 3.1–21 | 45 |
| 3.8–9 | 71, 79 |
| 16.1–13 | 71 |
| 16.7 | 46 |
| 16.10–13 | 79 |
| 16.11, 12, 13 | 46 |
| 17.25, 26 | 47 |
| 17.33 | 46 |
| 17.34–37 | 47 |
| 17.37 | 46, 71 |

| | | | |
|---|---|---|---|
| 17.42, 55, 58 | 46 | 59 | 130 |
| 17.45 | 47 | 61 | 130 |
| 17.46–47 | 47 | 78.4 | 43 |
| 17.55, 58 | 46 | 92.12–15 | 33 |
| | | 92.14 | 6 |
| *2 Samuel* | | 139.13–14 | 19 |
| 2.4 | 46 | 145.4 | 43 |
| *1 Kings* | | *Proverbs* | |
| 17.8–16 | 49, 50 | 1.89 | 92 |
| 19.1–18 | 123 | 4.1–5 | 92 |
| *2 Kings* | | *Isaiah* | |
| 5.1–5a | 71 | 6.2 | 14 |
| 5.3, 15 | 48 | 11.1–9 | 8, 9, 11, 12 |
| *2 Chronicles* | | *Jeremiah* | |
| 20.13 | 44 | 17.7–8 | 33 |
| 20.15–17 | 44 | | |
| | | *Joel* | |
| *Nehemiah* | | 2.15, 16 | 44 |
| 12.43 | 44 | 2.28 | 58 |
| *Psalms* | | *Jonah* | |
| 1.1–3 | 33 | 2 | 130 |
| 8.5 | 8 | 3.10 | 123 |
| 57 | 130 | 4.1–11 | 123 |

## New Testament

| | | | |
|---|---|---|---|
| *Matthew* | | 17.1–8 | 128 |
| 5.2–12 | 126 | 17.10–13 | 29 |
| 13.1–9 | 33 | 18.1–5 | 96 |
| 13.18–23 | 33 | 18.1–14 | 9, 10, 14 |
| 13.31–32 | 33 | 18.4, 5 | 11, 12, 14 |
| 15.21–28 | 123 | 19.13–15 | 15 |

# INDEX OF BIBLICAL REFERENCES

| | | | |
|---|---|---|---|
| 19.29 | 95 | **John** | |
| 21.1 | 128 | 3.3, 4 | 10 |
| 26.36–46 | 130 | 5.6–8 | 123 |
| 28.16–20 | 129 | 6.5–14 | 49, 50, 71 |
| | | 11.21–44 | 123 |
| **Mark** | | 15.1–17 | 33 |
| 4.3–9 | 33 | | |
| 4.26–29 | 33 | **Acts** | |
| 9.30–33 | 96 | 2.14–21 | 58 |
| 9.33–37 | 9, 96 | 2.42 | 41, 72 |
| 9.37 | 12 | | |
| 9.42–48 | 9 | **Romans** | |
| 10.13–16 | 15 | 6.4 | 122 |
| 10.14 | 11 | 8.4–16 | 40 |
| 10.15 | 96 | 12.2 | 122 |
| 10.29–30 | 95 | 12.4–5 | 39 |
| 11.1 | 128 | 12.10 | 41 |
| 14.32–42 | 130 | 15.26 | 41, 79 |
| | | | |
| **Luke** | | **1 Corinthians** | |
| 1.46–55 | 130 | 1.9 | 40 |
| 1.64 | 130 | 10.16 | 40 |
| 1.67–79 | 130 | 12.13 | 39 |
| 2.41–51 | 68n3 | 12.12–31 | 39 |
| 5.1–11 | 126 | | |
| 6.20–23 | 126 | **2 Corinthians** | |
| 9.28–36 | 128 | 3.18 | 122 |
| 9.46–48 | 9, 12 | 5.17 | 122 |
| 10.25–37 | 62 | 8.4 | 41 |
| 15.3–7 | 9 | 9.13 | 41 |
| 17.1–2 | 9 | 13.13 | 40 |
| 18.15–17 | 15 | | |
| 18.29–30 | 95 | **Galatians** | |
| 22.39–53 | 129, 130 | 2.9 | 41, 72, 79 |
| | | 3.28 | 39 |
| | | 6.10 | 41 |

*Ephesians*

| | |
|---|---|
| 1.20–23 | 39 |
| 2.11–22 | 42 |
| 2.19–20 | 39 |
| 4.3 | 4 |
| 4.12, 15, 16 | 39 |
| 5.22—6.9 | 101 |
| 6.1 | 96 |

*Philippians*

| | |
|---|---|
| 2.1 | 40 |
| 4.8 | 63 |

*Colossians*

| | |
|---|---|
| 1.18 | 39 |
| 2.19 | 39 |
| 3.14 | 41 |
| 3.14–16 | 39 |
| 3.18—4.1 | 101 |

*1 Thessalonians*

| | |
|---|---|
| 1.1 | 40 |
| 3.12 | 41 |
| 5.15 | 41 |
| 5.15–18 | 63 |

*1 Timothy*

| | |
|---|---|
| 6.18 | 41 |

*Hebrews*

| | |
|---|---|
| 11.1 | 18 |

www.ingramcontent.com/pod-product-compliance
Lightning Source LLC
Chambersburg PA
CBHW022016290426
44109CB00015B/1184